Classical Studies

Discovering the Greeks

P Kenneth Corsar
Niall MacKinnon
Andrew Reid
James Rooney
Robert S Smith

Drawings by Philip M L Page MA

Hodder & Stoughton

A MEMBER OF THE HODDER HEADLINE GROUP

ISBN 0 7131 0033 8

First published 1977
Impression number   15 14 13 12
Year   1999   1998   1997   1996

Printed in Great Britain for Hodder & Stoughton Educational,
a division of Hodder Headline Plc, 338 Euston Road,
London NW1 3BH by Redwood Books, Trowbridge, Wiltshire.

Preface

This book is designed to present a detailed, yet easy to read, account of Greek life, mainly in Classical times. The book is primarily intended for pupils in the lower forms of secondary schools, but can also be used with pupils in middle schools and upper forms of primary schools. Flexibility has been one of our aims, and comments from those who have assisted with the testing of the material suggest that, to a considerable extent, this has been achieved. We intend the book to provide education in the broadest possible sense of the word; at the same time we sincerely hope that this book will be seen as a foundation course, upon which may be built more detailed courses leading to Classical Studies examinations.

The objectives of the book are simply stated:

1 to make it possible for pupils to acquire a body of knowledge about Ancient Greece, using, where possible, original source material;
2 to use this knowledge as a basis for promoting the idea that much of modern civilization stems from Ancient Greece;
3 to provide attractive worksheets which will stress the main points of information and give pupils a wide choice of activities, bearing in mind the needs of the teacher faced with a mixed-ability class;
4 to introduce new activity ideas, such as creative writing and art work, into Classics teaching.

Another of our hopes is that the book will be very suitable for the non-classicist who has the task of teaching Classical Studies. At the same time, it may be that classicists in particular will feel that on some topics too little information is given; if so, this is good, because we would like this book to be used as a basis for further work by teachers and pupils. One of the most obvious ways in which teachers will amplify the material is by the use of more illustrations; we have attempted to include as many and as vivid illustrations as we could, but it is our intention that teachers will use along with this book whatever stock they themselves have built up of illustrations, filmstrips, slides, pictures, wall-charts, posters, etc.

The work sections are divided into two parts; it will normally be desirable for all pupils to complete the first section, since it contains mainly factual exercises, designed to ensure that the pupils have a grasp of the basic information. In the second part, however, it is by no means essential for every pupil to attempt every question; the aim has been to produce a wide range of suggested activities, which will stimulate pupils of differing ability to undertake further research on their own.

It is obvious that small teaching sections are preferable for work of a practical nature. We do, however, feel that project work and practical activities can be undertaken successfully with larger groups, but obviously only if proper, detailed planning is undertaken. Some teachers will shy away from work of a practical nature on the grounds of limited or nonexistent artistic ability. There is no need to do so. Most pupils are only too willing to try practical work, and some of them, once given the basic idea, will make good progress on their own with very little help. Sometimes a better understanding can be established between pupil and teacher if the teacher openly admits that he is limited at practical work, and then tries to work and learn along with the pupil. The experience of finding out together (almost on an equal basis), can be very rewarding. Even if a piece of practical work is not particularly successful, at least the pupil (and the teacher) will have enjoyed making the effort.

Our indebtedness to many people is great. First we must thank our colleagues past and present, mainly in Dunbartonshire (as was), who got the idea off the ground and helped at various stages with criticisms, suggestions and encouragement. Particular mention must be made of J. Murray Allan, Esq., who, as Senior Depute Director of Education in Dunbartonshire with responsibility for secondary curriculum development when the project began, gave it a great amount of impetus by his co-operation and suggestions. It would be impossible to mention individually all those who assisted with mundane matters like typing at the various stages of production; without their freely given help our task would have been almost impossible; everyone's efforts, big or small, are greatly appreciated. We are equally indebted to all who have given permission to use quotations, illustrations and photographs which are such a vital part of the book.

Contents

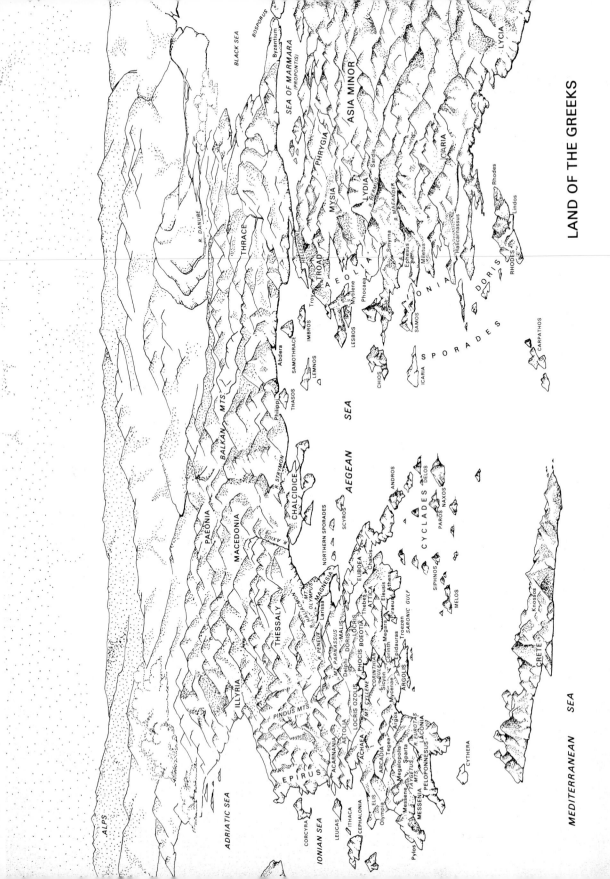

LAND OF THE GREEKS

1 Hellas-The Land of the Greeks

Greece is a land of rocky mountains and dry, dusty earth. For a few weeks in Spring it looks fresh and green; but soon, as the sun blazes relentlessly from a cloudless sky, the rivers dry up and most of the vegetation is burned brown except the pine and the all-important olive, upon which the Greeks have always greatly depended.

The winters in Greece are cold and often, even in Spring, the mountain tops have a covering of snow. Two other striking features of the land of the Greeks are the sea inlets, which penetrate far into the land, and the vast number of islands scattered off its eastern coast.

The mountains of Greece

In ancient times, these mountains, inlets and islands together made communication among the Greeks themselves very difficult indeed and on the mainland this resulted in the formation of small independent communities almost completely cut off, one from another. These became known as city-states and each included a small city and the land and villages around it.

Each city-state had its own government and laws, but throughout the country the people spoke the same language and worshipped the same gods in whose honour national festivals, such as the Olympic Games, were held. It was only on such occasions that the Greeks really united.

The most important of these city-states were Attica (with its main city of Athens), Sparta, Corinth, Thebes, Delphi and Olympia; but they were no larger than small country towns today and, generally speaking, they were neither rich nor powerful.

Each city was usually built around the base of a rocky hill upon which there stood a fortress or 'acropolis', to give the citizens protection in times of danger. Also on this hill would be the temples dedicated to the gods who were thought to defend the city-state.

A city-state

As the populations grew, the boundaries of the city-states became too narrow. Around 700 BC many people, especially those who worked on the land, were forced to cross the uncharted seas to find new homes in what are now the countries of Turkey, Italy, France and Spain. These emigrants were often joined by people who were merely seeking adventure and together they founded colonies all round the Mediterranean coast. This resulted in an increase in Greek trading which in turn greatly improved the prosperity of the Greeks both at home and abroad. Wherever they settled, the Greeks clung to

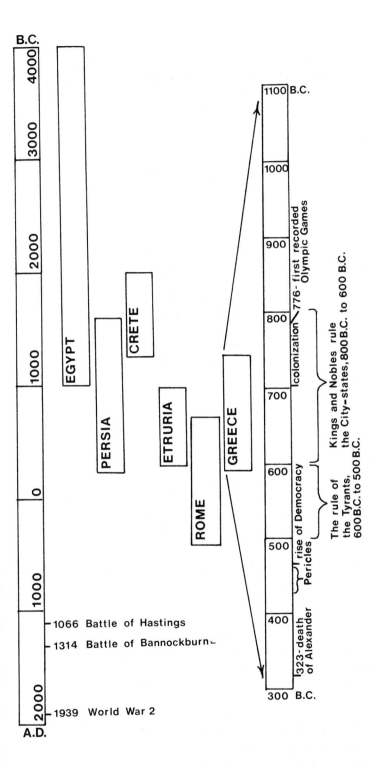

Time Chart

3

their original homeland and never thought of themselves as being anything other than Greek. 'It is a rough land,' said Ulysses, 'but a good nurse of men and I want no sweeter home.'

At first the city-states were ruled by kings, but gradually they were replaced by nobles, except in Sparta which continued to have kings. Usually, one noble, more powerful than the others, would gain the upper hand and become sole ruler or tyrant (just after 600 BC). Very often these tyrants ruled well. However, if a tyrant was harsh or weak, some city-states would forcibly remove him. Soon after 500 BC, democracies arose in which the people themselves ruled, each male citizen being allowed to participate in the assemblies which formed an important part of the government of the city-state.

The democracies of Ancient Greece would not have been so successful had it not been for the fact that all manual labour was done by slaves. Slaves mined in the hills around the cities for iron and precious metals. Slaves farmed the land, produced oil from the olive and wine from the vine, and tended the sheep and goats.

Thus the men of the city-states had a great deal of free time in which to attend the assemblies. Only the men went to the assemblies. The Greeks truly believed that a woman's place was in the home. With the exception of priestesses and temple dancers, no woman was allowed to play any part in public life.

Our debt to Greece

About the Ancient Greeks there is much that we cannot admire—they could not live harmoniously together, they depended to a great extent on slave labour, they disliked and distrusted foreigners; but Pericles, the great Athenian leader, was nevertheless correct when he said, 'Future ages will wonder at us as the present age wonders at us now.'

We wonder at them because they opened the eyes and minds of succeeding ages to the marvels of astronomy, to the precision of mathematics, to the miracles of medicine, the beauty and excitement of their art, architecture, poetry and drama. In addition, many of the roots of philosophy (the study of wisdom), of history (the recording of events) and democracy (rule by the people) all had their beginnings in Ancient Greece. Today, wherever we look, there are still signs of Greek influence. Many recent buildings like town halls, museums, government offices and schools have been modelled on Greek temples.

Museums display Greek statues, their distinctive, shiny black pottery and the furniture which adorned their homes.

Their plays are still performed in the theatre and their

The British Museum

literature is widely read (both mainly in translation), and many exciting adventure films are made about their heroes. The language of the Greeks is still studied in schools and universities and many of the letters of the Greek alphabet are used daily by scientists and mathematicians.

Without doubt our way of life has been enriched by the achievements of the Greeks.

'Mighty indeed are the marks and monuments . . . we have left.'

The Acropolis, Athens

The Parthenon, Athens

Things to do:

1 Trace the map of the Mediterranean area below and mark the Greek colonies. Try to mark the various countries on the map. Try also to find out the distance between Glasgow and Greece. The distance between Glasgow and London is around 400 miles.

2 Look at the timechart. How long ago from the present year is the start of the Second World War? How long ago from the present year is the Battle of Hastings? Many people believe the great era of Ancient Greece finished with the death of Alexander the Great in 323 BC. How long ago from the present year is this?

The Mediterranean area, showing Greek colonies

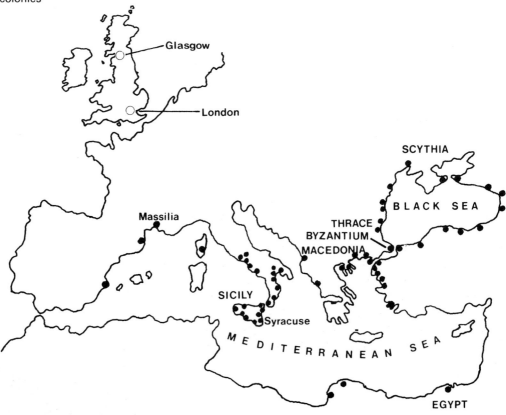

6

2 The Gods of Olympus

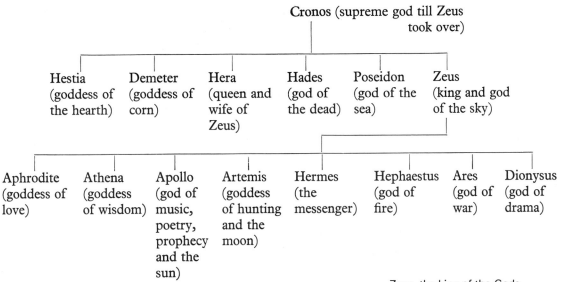

Cronos (supreme god till Zeus took over)

- Hestia (goddess of the hearth)
- Demeter (goddess of corn)
- Hera (queen and wife of Zeus)
- Hades (god of the dead)
- Poseidon (god of the sea)
- Zeus (king and god of the sky)

- Aphrodite (goddess of love)
- Athena (goddess of wisdom)
- Apollo (god of music, poetry, prophecy and the sun)
- Artemis (goddess of hunting and the moon)
- Hermes (the messenger)
- Hephaestus (god of fire)
- Ares (god of war)
- Dionysus (god of drama)

Zeus, the king of the Gods

The diagram shows the main Greek gods and goddesses. The Greeks believed that there were many gods and goddesses each of whom had special duties and responsibilities. They thought their gods and goddesses were like human beings both in appearance and attitude—they ate and drank, listened to music, fell in love and quarrelled. As the Greek poet, Xenophanes, said, 'Man made his gods and furnished them with his own body, voice and garments.' There was, however, one very important difference. The gods and goddesses were immortal.

Zeus ruled over the gods and goddesses who lived at the top of Mount Olympus, a mountain in the north of Greece. For this reason the gods and goddesses are sometimes called the Olympians. Zeus also ruled over mankind. His favourite weapon was the thunderbolt, and so, when people on the earth heard thunder and saw lightning, they thought Zeus was angry with someone.

We can begin to see from this how the gods and goddesses came into being. They were really powers of nature. The first Greeks had practically no knowledge of Science, and so, when they saw lightning flash and heard the sound of thunder, they thought there must be some power behind these happenings, some super-being—in other words some god. This is probably how Zeus arose. Apollo represents the power of the sun and his sister Artemis the power of the moon. Poseidon is the power behind the seas and their storms and also behind earthquakes. Homer describes him as the 'Girdler of Earth', and 'the Lord of the Earthquake'. Demeter represents the power of the earth to produce crops. The Greeks saw the wonderful powers of nature and concluded that there must be some god or goddess behind each one.

The Greeks believed the gods and goddesses influenced their daily lives and that it was an advantage to have them on their side. For this reason the Greeks built beautiful temples for the gods and goddesses, originally made of wood but later of stone. The most famous one is the Parthenon in Athens dedicated to Athena. Most temples had two rooms, the first one containing a statue of the particular god or goddess and the second sometimes being used as a store-room for valuables. Greek religion was, to a certain extent, like a business deal. Normally, if a person wanted to ask for something from a god or goddess, he would give a present, usually the sacrifice of some animal. This was always done at an altar, just outside the temple. The god or goddess received, as an offering, the blood which was

A sacrifice

8

sprinkled on the altar. The god or goddess also received the thigh-bones, which were wrapped in fat and burned on the altar. The remaining parts of the animal were cooked and eaten up by all the people at the sacrifice.

Once the sacrifice had been made, the person who wanted to consult the god or goddess would go into the interior of the temple and ask him or her to grant his wish. The relationship between the god or goddess and the worshipper in some ways resembled a business arrangement. The worshipper could argue, though always with the utmost respect, that he had given a payment and it was, therefore, only right that the god or goddess should give something in return. Greek temples were not used like churches where congregations sang hymns and prayed together. They were for private prayers.

Let us look now at some of the gods and goddesses individually.

Hera was the wife of Zeus and queen of heaven. She was the only married goddess and so is also worshipped as the goddess of marriage. She seems to have been very jealous and there are many references in Greek literature to her persecution of other women that Zeus had favoured.

Athena was the goddess of wisdom and crafts. The city of Athens is named after her and is the site of her most famous temple, the Parthenon.

Apollo was the son of Zeus and had many talents. He was the god of the sun, music, poetry and prophecy. It was as god of prophecy that he exercised most influence over the Greeks. All over Greece, and especially at Delphi, shrines were established to Apollo where the Greeks could go to ask about the future. Delphi was the most famous shrine, known as an oracle, and there was a special priestess of Apollo, called the Pythia, who would sit on a golden tripod above a crack in the earth. She breathed in fumes which came up through the crack, went into a trance and uttered the words of Apollo, who was supposed to be speaking through her. In this way, human beings thought they had been in touch with the god of prophecy.

Artemis was the daughter of Zeus and the goddess of hunting and the moon. It is because of her connection with hunting that you often see pictures of her with a bow and arrows. She was also the goddess of the night and the protectress of women. A great temple was built in her honour at Ephesus in Asia Minor and this became one of the seven Wonders of the Ancient World.

Demeter was the goddess of corn and country products. Persephone, her daughter, was desired by Hades, god of the dead, and was carried off by him. Demeter was very upset and

Hera, the Queen of Heaven

The Pythia at Delphi

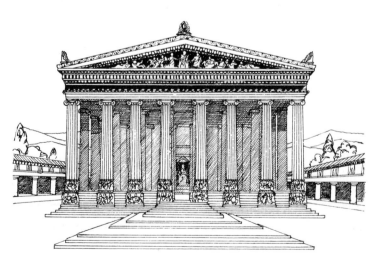

10 The temple of Artemis, Ephesus

The kidnap of Persephone

refused to let crops grow upon the earth until her daughter was restored. Hades, on the other hand, was very reluctant to let Persephone go. Zeus intervened and a settlement was made. Persephone was to spend seven months with Demeter and five with Hades. There is a connection with nature behind this story too. The five months that Persephone spends with Hades are the months when Demeter is unhappy and nothing is allowed to grow on the earth, in other words Winter. This is how the Greeks explained the changing seasons.

Hades, god of the Underworld

Hades was the god of the Underworld (the land of the dead). The Greeks believed that, when a person died, that person's ghost went there. If the person had been good, the ghost was sent to Elysium, where it enjoyed a wonderful existence. If, however, the person had been evil, the ghost was sent to Tartarus, where it suffered eternal torture.

Hermes was the messenger of the gods and goddesses. For this reason we often see pictures of him with winged shoes and a winged helmet. He was also the god of trade, luck and theft. His connection with theft goes back to his youth. He stole some of Apollo's cattle when he was just a few hours old.

Dionysus was the son of Zeus and the god of wine and drama. It is as god of drama that he is best remembered. In Athens there was a great dramatic festival in his honour held in his theatre. Dionysus was the youngest of the gods.

We have looked at the gods and goddesses briefly. Their importance must not be underestimated. As time passed some people became sceptical about them. Xenophanes says:

> The truth is that no man ever was or will be who understands the gods and all I speak of. If you stumble on some rocks of the whole truth you never know it. There is always speculation.

The normal Greek attitude, however, was to believe in the gods and goddesses and think 'the gods are everywhere'.

Hermes, messenger of the gods

Things to do:

1 Write out the following statements in your jotter, filling in the blanks:

    (a) Demeter was the goddess of.......

    (b) The queen of the gods and goddesses was.......

    (c) Hades was the god of the.......

    (d) The god of the sea was.......

    (e) Zeus was.......

    (f) The goddess of wisdom was.......

    (g) Artemis was.......

    (h) The god of prophecy was.......

2 Imagine that you are the leading citizen of Athens. Your city is about to fight a war. You have decided you want the goddess Athena to be on your side and to achieve this you are going to make her a sacrifice. Describe the full scene— the sacrifice outside the temple and what happens when you go inside.

3 The temple of Artemis at Ephesus was one of the seven Wonders of the Ancient World. Try to discover the other six and all you can about them.

4 Choose one of the gods and goddesses and do a drawing of him or her.

3 The Olympic Games-
Athletes and Heroes

Rome 1960, Tokyo 1964, Mexico City 1968, Munich 1972, Montreal 1976, Moscow 1980!

These places and dates will immediately bring to mind the Olympic Games, but what must be remembered is that we in the twentieth century did not begin the games. The Olympic Games have come down to us from the past, because, like much in our lives, they were born in Ancient Greece.

The first games for which there is any evidence took place in 776 BC. From this date until AD 396 the Olympics were held every four years at Olympia in southern Greece. There, temples and sports arenas were built on the ruins of an old city, and it was to this spot that athletes from all over the Greek world flocked for competition.

Before the games, heralds (or messengers) would visit every Greek city and invite free-born Greek citizens to come to

The stadium at Olympia

Olympia to take part. These heralds—'truce-bearers of Zeus'—were actually on a sort of divine mission, for the games were not only an athletic competition but part of a great religious festival in honour of the great god Zeus.

The statue of Zeus, Olympia

All fighting had to stop immediately, so that during their journeys by land and sea to Olympia and during the five days of the festival, everyone would be safe from war. We should remember that the Greeks were great colonists and had set up many outposts of Greek civilization all over the Mediterranean. So, many of the athletes faced a long journey to Olympia, some coming all the way from the Black Sea, which was a long and dangerous journey for them.

As the opening of the games drew near crowds of travellers, on their way to the games, filled the roads leading to Olympia. The athletes—men only, since women were not allowed to attend—arrived at Olympia about a month before the games began, so that they could complete their training under the supervision of the officials. A tent village would spring up, and the whole atmosphere would be one of gay carnival. There would be a fair, and there would be stalls where people could buy and sell their goods.

The games themselves, which were held in August or September, lasted only five days.

On *Day 1* a religious ceremony took place. A pig was sacrificed to Zeus, in whose honour the games were being held. All who were involved in the games took an oath, the athletes not to cheat and the judges to be completely fair in their decisions. Then a list of entries for each competition was made and the various heats were arranged. All events in the ancient Olympics were contested by individuals; there were no team contests as in modern times.

Day 2 began with a procession. It was led by the officials of the games who were dressed in fine purple robes, but everyone involved in the competitions paraded, accompanied by the horses and chariots.

The first event was for four-horse chariots and took place in the Hippodrome. It was a nine-mile race, which meant twelve laps of the course. The technique of driving in a race of this kind was to turn round the pillars at each end of the course as closely as possible and without losing too much speed. This, of course, led to frequent accidents and collisions, which also meant that this was a very popular event with the spectators.

The sacrifice of a pig

The Chariot Race

After the chariot race came a jockeys' race or horse-race. This also took place in the Hippodrome and lasted only one lap. The jockey had to be very skilful as he rode bare-back without saddle or stirrups.

One of the most important events in the whole of the games was also held on the second day. It was the Pentathlon, a combination of five different events—running, long-jump, discus, javelin and wrestling. The Pentathlon was a contest for the all-round athlete, and only the best could hope to win. Let us look at each of the five events separately.

15

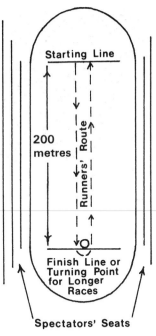

Starting Line

200 metres

Runners' Route

Finish Line or Turning Point for Longer Races

Spectators' Seats

Plan of the stadium *(above)*

The Pentathlon *(above right)*

The starting line, Olympia

The running events were held in the Stadium, so called because its length was one 'stadion' or 200 metres. The competitors raced up and down the track and not round it as we do today. The starter had no gun or whistle, but instead had a stick with which he used to beat any runner who started too soon. The track was covered with white sand. At Olympia today you can still see the starting and finishing line, consisting of stone slabs, about 45 centimetres wide, set right across the course. In these slabs, parallel grooves were set about $17\frac{1}{2}$ centimetres apart, which appear as if they had been used by runners to get a toe-grip. They probably served the same purpose as starting blocks do today.

The runners and most of the other athletes wore no distinguishing coloured vests or running-shoes. They contested all events, except chariot races, in the nude. To the Greeks nudity was natural, and physical fitness was something to be proud of, while being flabby and fat was considered shameful. The story is told that in an early contest a competitor lost his shorts during a race and this made the Greeks realize that it was easier to run without any clothing at all.

The long-jump may have been similar to ours, or may have been a hop, step and jump, but in Ancient Greece the jumpers were allowed to use weights. The athlete held these in his hands and swung them forward to gain impetus and increase the length of his jump. It seems that the performance of ancient Greek long-jumpers compared favourably with many modern leaps. (As far as is known, the Greeks had no high-jump event.)

Discus throwing was one of the oldest and most popular sports in Greece. The disc was made of stone or of a metal like bronze, and could weigh from 1½ to 4 kilograms. The object of this event, as today, was to throw the disc as far as possible. The discus was held above the head, then swung down in the right hand, and back again on the forward swing, to be thrown with all the weight of the body behind it. The picture shows the moment when the discus has been swung back, and is just about to be thrown forward again.

Another throwing event was the javelin. This event may have started off as part of a scheme to keep men fit for spear-throwing in war.

Wrestling, the final event of the Pentathlon, is one of the oldest of all sports. With the Greeks a fall on any part of the body counted. If both wrestlers fell, there was no count. Three falls were enough for victory, and tripping was allowed.

The Pentathlon was the last event of *Day 2*.

Day 3 provided a rest for the men. There were more religious ceremonies, and then several junior events for boys, mainly wrestling, boxing and running. Boxers did not wear gloves, but they tied leather strips round their hands to protect their knuckles. There were no rounds and no division into 'weights'. A match continued until one of the competitors gave in.

On *Day 4* there were more foot races. As well as short sprints,

Long Jump

Javelin *(left)*

Discus *(below)*

17

Wrestling *(above left and right)*

The Pankration

the Greeks had races of 7, 12, 20, 24 stades in length. This day also saw the event called Pankration. This was perhaps the toughest, hardest event; wrestling, strangling, arm-twisting, hitting, kicking and jumping on an opponent were all allowed, as in the boxing practised in Thailand or Japan. Everything seemed possible except biting and gouging out the eyes. Men sometimes died in the Pankration.

There was also a race in armour. The runners wearing helmets and carrying round shields raced over a distance of two stades. One of the reasons why the Greeks placed such emphasis on physical fitness was because of the fact that they might be called on at any time to defend their city in war, and the race in armour is a reminder of that very fact.

The race in armour

Day 5, the last day of the festival, was a social occasion. The winners received their prizes—not gold, silver or bronze medals as today—but a crown of wild olive cut from the trees growing in a sacred grove near the temple of Zeus. Later they were treated to a victory banquet, and the festival ended with all the athletes parading in the moonlight, singing hymns.

An Olympic victor was sure of a great reception when he arrived home. Everyone would turn out to see him. His fellow

The victor, wearing his olive crown

citizens would cheer him and congratulate him on his victory. Think of the great crowds which turn up to see a cup-winning football team in either Scotland or England when the team returns home, and you will be able to imagine the atmosphere. The name of the victor would be recorded in a golden book, and he would be allowed to wear purple robes like a king. He would not have to pay taxes, he would receive free meals in the town hall and the best seats at the theatre during a dramatic festival. A poem might be composed in his honour, and sometimes (especially if he had won three events) a statue would be erected to him at Olympia. With such fame and reward it is not surprising that every Greek man cherished a burning ambition to win at the Olympic Games.

Things to do:

Section A

Rewrite the following sentences and fill in the blanks by choosing the correct answer from the choices given or by supplying an answer.

1 The Olympics began in Greece in.......
   (a) Athens, (b) Sparta, (c) Olympia, (d) Olympus.

2 The games were held in honour of ....
   (a) Apollo, (b) Zeus, (c) Poseidon, (d) Dionysus

3 The games lasted ....
   (a) 5 days, (b) 1 month, (c) 3 weeks, (d) all summer

4 The hippodrome was used for ....
   (a) javelin, (b) race in armour, (c) chariot-racing, (d) wrestling

5 The Pentathlon consisted of ....
   (a) ten events, (b) two events, (c) five events, (d) twelve events.

6 The length of the running track was one stade which is
   ....
   (a) 200 metres, (b) 100 metres, (c) 440 metres, (d) 880 metres.

7 The Greek name 'stade' gives us the English word .... another name for an arena.

8 In the long jump, to help them jump further, athletes used ....
   (a) jumping-weights, (b) a discus, (c) stones.

9 One of the modern events not included in the ancient games was ....
   (a) the long jump, (b) the high jump, (c) throwing the discus, (d) throwing the javelin.

10 The Pankration was a kind of ...*hardest event.*

11 The prize for a victory in the games was a ....
(a) crown of wild olives, (b) sum of money, (c) medal,
(d) horse.

Section B

1 Describe the opening scene of the ancient Olympics.
What is the opening ceremony like in the modern games?

2 Imagine you are an Athenian who has won an event in the
Olympics. Describe the contest, the prize-giving ceremony,
the banquet and the welcome you receive on returning to
your city.

3 Design either a programme for the five days of the ancient
games or a poster to advertise the games.

4 Which events in the Ancient games are still to be found in
the modern ones?

5 The symbol of the modern Olympics is like this:

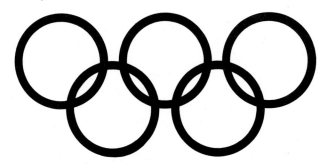

Copy it into your jotter or workbook. Try to find out what
it represents.

6 The ideal of the Olympic Games is 'It is better to compete
than to win.' Do you think this is true of modern sport?

21

4 The Greek Theatre

The theatre at Epidaurus

Have you ever been to the theatre? 'Theatre' is a word we have borrowed from Greek, as are many other words connected with acting, like scenery, chorus, orchestra, tragedy, comedy and drama. Many of these have, however, changed their meanings, as we shall see.

The performance of plays in Ancient Greece began as a festival in honour of the god Dionysus, god of wine and merriment. These festivals were held all over Greece; for example, there was one every year in Athens, held in March. The Theatre of Dionysus in Athens was dug out of the side of the Acropolis, but there were many similar theatres all over Greece, and some, like the famous one at Epidauros, are still used for the performance of plays today.

As you can see, a Greek theatre was almost circular, and it was normally cut out of a hillside to give descending rows of seats: the front seats were for the people who were chosen to judge the plays and for other distinguished people like Olympic victors or guests from other states, or priests. Immediately in front of the first row of seats was the orchestra, a flat circular space with an altar to Dionysus in the centre. On either side of the orchestra was a passageway called a parodos, which provided access to the orchestra. If the actors appeared from one side, the audience understood that they had come from the town;

Dionysus

The theatre of Dionysus, Athens

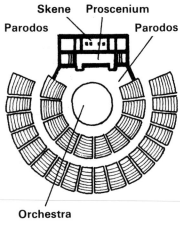

Skene Proscenium

Parodos Parodos

Orchestra

Reconstruction of a Greek theatre

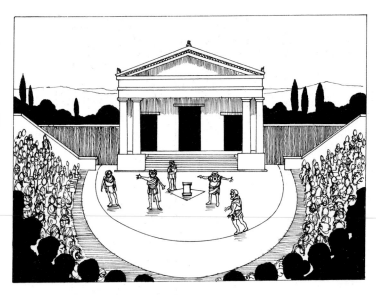

The chorus

if they came from the other side, they were supposed to have come from the country.

The orchestra was a dancing-floor where the members of the chorus of the play danced and sang. Beyond it was the stage (proscenium), really just a long, low platform with a building (skene) behind it which served as the scenery (normally representing the front of a palace) and also provided changing rooms. The whole theatre was entirely open to the sky.

In addition to being a religious festival in honour of Dionysus, the performance of plays was also a competition for the best-written and best-produced plays. These competitions lasted at least three days, and three dramatists were chosen to take part. Each dramatist had to produce four plays, three tragedies and a light-hearted play known as a satyr-play.

Comedies were also performed at some point in the festivals; they were, of course, very amusing. The writer of the best comedies, the writer of the best tragedies and the best actor all received a prize, probably a garland of ivy.

Each dramatist was allocated a choregus or sponsor—a wealthy citizen who met the expense of producing the plays in the theatre. This duty was considered an honour and was also an alternative way for the rich to pay their taxes.

The choregus had to collect a chorus and a teacher for them, arrange to have the chorus trained, and give a dinner to the performers in the plays for which he was responsible; the choregus who produced the best play received a prize.

The chorus training

Tragic and comic actors

There were normally only three actors in a play, all of whom would be men; each of them would play more than one part. The actors wore costumes, and, in tragedies, thick padding, very high-soled boots and high wigs to make them appear bigger and more impressive. The other important piece of equipment was their mask; masks were used to portray fixed types of expression like anger, joy, fear, happiness. These masks helped the audience, some of whom were high in the theatre and quite a distance from the stage, to identify the characters; they also enabled the actors to play more than one part.

At the beginning of the play a group of fifteen to twenty people led by a flute-player came on to the orchestra; at certain points in the play they sang and danced. They were the chorus, and in their songs they commented on the characters in the play and what they were doing.

Masks *(above)*

Actor in dressing room *(above right)*

As we have seen, the actual scenery in a Greek theatre was very simple. Various devices were, however, used to help the action of the play. For example, the middle section of the front of the skene may have been hinged to allow it to swivel.

This meant that a kind of platform could be brought on stage, probably to show, where necessary, something that was going on 'inside' the palace; alternatively a small platform on rails may have been wheeled from inside the skene for the same purpose. Another device may have been a kind of crane used to lower the gods from 'heaven' or take characters up to 'heaven'.

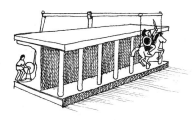

Stage crane

The Greeks also employed various sound effects, like the clapping together of wooden dishes for horses' hooves, or stones in an earthenware dish for rain; the chorus too, in their songs, often produced sound effects, like the sound of frogs croaking in a famous comedy.

The Great Dionysia was the festival in honour of Dionysus held in Athens each year. As soon as it was daylight, on each of the three chief days (which were public holidays) the citizens, rich and poor alike, flocked into the theatre of Dionysus, on the slopes of the Acropolis. They would bring with them their wives and families and they would all have a picnic lunch, since, for the men at least, the performances lasted all day; they might also be carrying cushions to make the benches a little more comfortable. They had to pay a small sum of money for admission, in return for which they received their 'ticket', a small stone disc, examples of which have been unearthed in theatres. If anyone was too poor to pay, he was allowed in free of charge.

The audience in a Greek theatre was not slow to react to the action that was taking place on the stage and in the orchestra. A good, well-acted play was greatly appreciated; the audience were liable to get carried away and become involved in the plot of the play as it unfolded; they would sway in time to the rhythm of the chorus's songs, weep at the misfortunes of the hero or be filled with fear as they witnessed the power of the gods.

On the other hand they were as quick at showing their disapproval of a bad actor or of one who could not be heard; they would whistle and shuffle their feet or even pelt him with whatever they could lay their hands on. The story is told of one actor who pronounced his lines so badly that at one point in the play where he should have said 'After the storm I see a calm' he seemed to say 'After the storm I see a cat'. The audience immediately burst into laughter at his unfortunate mistake. Similarly, if a play was not a very good one, the audience might become so noisy and violent that the performance was stopped. It was also possible for the audience to become bored by a play; in one of the famous Greek comedies, the author advocates the advantages of wings in such a situation:

Truly to be clad in feathers is the very best of things.
Only fancy, dear spectators, had you each a brace of wings,
Never need you, tired and hungry, at a Tragic Chorus
   stay;

27

You would lightly, when it bored you, spread your wings
    and fly away,
Back returning, after luncheon, to enjoy our Comic Play.

After spending a whole morning watching a set of three tragedies, the audience had a break for lunch; after this the women and children went home—the Greeks did not think comedies suitable for them—but the men stayed on to watch the comedy which was usually staged in the afternoon.

We still have some of the plays of three of the great Greek writers of tragedies. *Aeschylus* was the earliest; he fought in the great war of the Greeks against the Persians, and amongst his tragedies is one entitled 'The Persians' which showed how the Persian king was punished by the gods. *Sophocles* was a little younger than Aeschylus; he was also a soldier and statesman; we know that he wrote more than a hundred plays and won many prizes for them. *Euripides* is the name of the third writer. Their plays were all written between 500 and 400 BC. The subject of most of them was the old stories and legends about the gods and heroes.

Some of the subjects dealt with in Greek tragedies are problems which people still argue about. Is it wrong to break the law even if we think the law is unjust? Should we obey the government or our own conscience? Must we obey a king if what he asks us to do do is wicked? Should the young always obey their elders? These are the very questions which Sophocles placed before the audience in his play 'Antigone'.

Antigone's brothers had killed one another in single combat for the throne of Thebes. Creon, the new king of Thebes, decreed that one brother, Eteocles, should be buried with great honour, but that the other, Polyneices, who was regarded as a traitor, should be left unburied. Anyone who tried to bury him was to be put to death.

Antigone disagrees with Creon. The gods say that people must respect the dead, whatever they have done; so she buries the body. She is arrested and brought before the king; she does not try to deny what she has done, but believes that she had to do what her conscience told her was right, although this meant defying the king's law; she is ready to die for what she believes to be right. She tells Creon

For me to meet death is easy; but if I had allowed my mother's son to lie dead, an unburied corpse, that would have grieved me; and if what I do now is foolish in your eyes, perhaps it is because a foolish judge is passing sentence on my folly.

Creon is furious; although Antigone is engaged to be married

A scene from a modern performance of 'Antigone'

28

to his son, who pleads with him to spare Antigone's life, he stubbornly refuses to listen.

Will men of my age be told what to do by men of his age?

So Antigone is led away to her death. But as the play goes on, we see that it is Creon who was wrong. Because he thought his laws were greater than the laws of the gods, he is punished terribly. His wife and son die, and at the end of the play he is a sad and lonely man.

Lead me away, I beg you, a rash, foolish man; I have killed you, my son, although I did not know it, and you too, my wife, unhappy that I am. I do not know which way to turn or where to seek support.

The chorus end the play by pointing out the moral—

The greatest gifts a man can have are wisdom and the fear of the gods. The great words of a boastful man are always punished with great blows and they are taught wisdom in their old age.

The only writer of comedies whose plays have survived was called Aristophanes. He chose as his themes well-known people and happenings of his own times and ridiculed them. One of his plays, 'The Birds' describes an adventure of two Athenians who, in order to escape the problems of living on earth, set out to find the kingdom of the birds. It was probably intended to make fun of certain politicians of his day and their over-ambitious schemes. When the two heroes eventually discover the advantages of living among the birds, they decide to build a city in mid-air and call it 'Cloud-cuckoo-burgh'. This scheme incurs the anger of the gods since the smell of sacrifices from mortals is blocked from them; so they send a deputation to come to terms with the heroes. The whole play is extremely amusing.

Many of the plays of these Greek writers have been translated into modern languages and are still performed. Perhaps you will have the chance to see some of them one day.

A scene from a modern performance of 'Antigone'

29

Things to do:

Section A

1 How did the performance of plays probably begin?
2 Make a diagram of a Greek theatre: Mark the following:
(i) Skene (ii) Proscenium (iii) Parodos (iv) Orchestra (v) Rows of seats
Under your diagram write a sentence to explain what each of i–iv were.
3 Write the heading *Dramatic Festivals*. Copy and complete these sentences:
(a) These festivals lasted for at least . . . .
(b) . . . . dramatists took part.
(c) Each dramatist had to produce . . . . tragedies and . . . .
(d) A prize of . . . . was awarded to the writers of the best plays and . . . .
(e) There were usually . . . . actors in a play. They were all . . . .
4 Write the heading *The Chorus*. Under it write a short paragraph to explain what the chorus was and what it did. In another short paragraph do the same for the heading *Choregus*.
5 Draw and colour, if possible, a tragic and a comic actor. Mark on your drawing the various items of their equipment.
6 Copy some of the actor's masks which are shown on pages 25 and 26. Say what feeling you think each represents. Why did actors wear masks?

Section B

1 Imagine yourself as a producer of a play in an ancient theatre. What difficulties do you think there would be in staging a play?
2 'Antigone' is a popular play even today. Why do you think that this is so?
3 It is not difficult to make a model of a Greek theatre, using very simple materials. On the opposite page there is a diagram to help you.

GREEK THEATRE

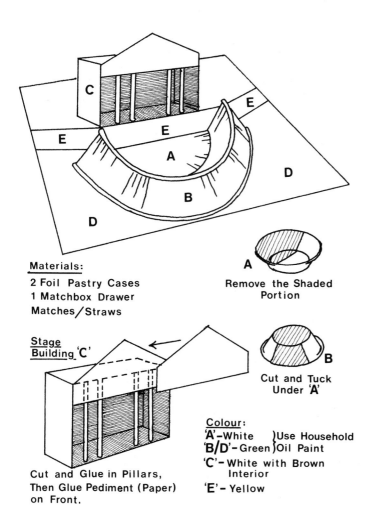

Materials:
2 Foil Pastry Cases
1 Matchbox Drawer
Matches/Straws

A
Remove the Shaded
Portion

<u>Stage
Building</u> 'C'

B
Cut and Tuck
Under 'A'

Cut and Glue in Pillars,
Then Glue Pediment (Paper)
on Front.

<u>Colour:</u>
'A'-White)Use Household
'B/D'-Green)Oil Paint
'C'-White with Brown
   Interior
'E'- Yellow

5 The Alphabet

At first the Greeks had no alphabet at all, and therefore they could not write things down. They found this a handicap and, as a result, they adopted the Minoan signs which had been developed in Crete. On the left is an example of this script. Archaeologists have given it the name 'Linear B.' After this in the eighth century BC Greek merchants in Syria, at the eastern end of the Mediterranean, brought back the Phoenician alphabet which was simpler, and this replaced the Minoan one. In fact, the Greeks added to it because they put in more signs for vowels and they wrote it from left to right as we do, instead of the opposite way as the Phoenicians had done. The Romans who gave us our alphabet got many of their letters from the Greeks.

Linear B tablet

The alphabet

Capital	Simple	Name	English
A	α	alpha	a
B	β	beta	b
Γ	γ	gamma	g
Δ	δ	delta	d
E	ε	epsilon	short e
Z	ζ	zeta	z
H	η	eta	long e
Θ	θ	theta	th
I	ι	iota	i
K	κ	kappa	k
Λ	λ	lambda	l
M	μ	mu	m
N	ν	nu	n
Ξ	ξ	xi	x
O	ο	omicron	short o
Π	π	pi	p

P	ρ	rho	r
Σ	$\sigma\varsigma$	sigma	s
T	τ	tau	t
Y	υ	upsilon	u
Φ	ϕ	phi	ph
X	χ	chi	ch
Ψ	ψ	psi	ps
Ω	ω	omega	long o

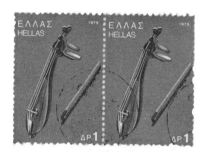

The Greeks expressed an h at the beginning of a word by using a rough breathing, e.g. ‘$E\lambda\lambda\alpha\varsigma$ = Hellas (Greece).

Many everyday words, including drama, tragedy, atom, Bible, and school, have been taken from ancient Greek. The actual letters of the alphabet are also in common use—physics teachers, for instance, refer to alpha, beta and gamma particles; one of the commonest mathematical symbols is the letter π; a delta-winged aircraft gets its name because the shape of the wings is like the capital of the fourth letter of the Greek alphabet. For the same reason a river mouth that spreads itself out into different channels, like the Nile or the Mississippi, is also called a delta.

Things to do:

1 Copy the table of the alphabet into your jotter.
2 Copy the following sentences into your jotter and try to complete them correctly:
  (a) The Greek letter most commonly used in Mathematics is .... and it is used in the formula .... d to find the length of the circumference of a circle.
  (b) A river mouth that spreads itself out is called a ....
  (c) Our word alphabet comes from the names of the first two letters of the Greek alphabet, ... and ....
3 It is amazing how many names of subjects you study in school come from Greek words. Below you are given the Greek word and what it means. Copy these into your jotter, then write down the English equivalents of the Greek letters and discover the subjects.
  $\gamma\eta$ (earth) and $\gamma\rho\alpha\phi\omega$ (I write down)
  ge   grapho   = geography

  $\beta\iota o\varsigma$ (life) and $\lambda o\gamma o\varsigma$ (study)
  $\gamma\eta$ (earth) and $\mu\epsilon\tau\rho o\nu$ (a measure)
  $\alpha\rho\iota\theta\mu\eta\tau\iota\kappa\eta$ (counting)
  $\iota\sigma\tau o\rho\iota\alpha$ (account of one's enquiries)

33

4 Many other very common words in English come from Greek. When some of the Greek words come into English they have different meanings. Below you are given the Greek forms. Where there is a difference in meaning, the original meaning is given. Copy these Greek words into your jotter and from them work out the English words we have today.

σχολη (leisure)
schole = school

βιβλος (book)
δραμα
τραγωδια
ατομος
αστρον (star) and ναυτης (sailor)
πεντε (five) and αθλον (contest)
δεκα (ten) and αθλον
αστρον and νομος (law)
αστρον and λογος
αρχαιος (old) and λογος
δημος (people) and κρατος (power)
ἱππος (horse) and ποταμος (river)

5 Many of our Christian names come from Greek. Copy out the following and see if you can discover their English forms.

γεωργος (farmer)
georgos = George

πετρα (rock)
φιλιππος (horse-lover)
αλεξανδρος (helper of men)
ανδρειος (manly)
βασιλευς (king)
καθαρος (pure)
ειρηνη (peace)
δωρον (gift) and θεος (god)
ἑλενη (torch)

6 The early Christians used Greek symbols to identify each other because their religion was banned. You may have seen the symbol ⳩ which is the first two letters of χριστος a Greek word meaning 'anointed'. Try to work out why this symbol was used.

7 Try to write your name and the place where you live in Greek. Here is an example—*Ριχαρδ Σμιθ, Σκοτλανδ.*
It should be done according to pronunciation. Once this has been checked it could be written out again in colour and stuck to the cover of your jotter.

34

6 Sparta

We, today, owe a great debt to Ancient Greece. It was there, in the various city-states (and especially in Athens), that the foundations were laid for our civilization and our way of life—our arts, our science, even our politics and our way of thinking. Sparta, however, differs strikingly from any other city in Ancient Greece. This city has left us nothing except the reputation for having the finest army in Greece. Everything there was geared for one thing—war. The reason for this goes back a long way.

The early descendants of the Spartans had come from the bleak northern regions of Greece and settled in the south, in the fertile valley of the river Eurotas, which lay in the district of Laconia. The Spartans soon came to dominate all of Laconia, conquering the original inhabitants of the area. They ruled over many towns and villages. In a few of these the people kept some personal freedom, and were allowed to trade or farm their own plots of land. These people were called Perioikoi, or neighbours. Although they were occasionally liable for military duty and subject to a heavy tax, many of them prospered. Others were not so lucky. Those who had resisted the Spartan conquest too fiercely were forced to become slaves, entirely at the mercy of their Spartan masters. These people, called Helots, were probably worse off than any other people in Greece. They were regarded not so much like human beings as like pieces of property. They were forced to work long, hard hours and to hand over everything they produced to their masters. They were beaten if they did not work hard enough and murdered if they protested. Living off the labours of others and adding the neighbouring lands of Messenia to their conquests, the Spartans became one of the richest nations in Greece. They seemed to have been a pleasure-loving people, and they produced poets and artists of high quality.

The Spartans were ruled over by two kings, probably the result of joining two kingdoms together in their early days,

Helots at work in the fields

A Helot is beaten by his Spartan master

Men of the Gerousia in debate

although the Greek historian Herodotus says that this system started when a Spartan queen gave birth to twins and refused to say which one had been born first! In peace the power of the kings was limited and they were assisted in running the state by the Gerousia—a council of twenty-eight senior citizens, men over sixty years old. In fact, this council discussed and decided nearly all matters of state. Their decisions were submitted to an assembly of all the citizens—the Apella—but the power of this assembly was very slight: the citizens could say only 'Yes' or 'No' to any proposal and they were not permitted to make any changes. The 'Yes'/'No' votes were not even counted properly. Instead, a small group of men was set aside in a separate room and they had to decide which group—the 'Yesses' or the 'Noes'—had shouted loudest! In times of war the kings reigned supreme. One would stay at home, while the other marched out at the head of a personal bodyguard of three hundred picked soldiers, directing the campaign with absolute authority.

Despite their wealth and power, the Spartans were never really secure. They always feared that the Helots, driven to desperation by their slavery, would rebel. In 650 BC this fear became a reality when the Helots did indeed rise up in revolt. Only after a long period of fierce fighting did the Spartans crush the Helots. They realized then that, if they were to keep control of a population of slaves who outnumbered the free citizens by about fifteen to one, they would have to reorganize the state to take account of only one thing—superb military efficiency and readiness for war. They turned their backs on their developing literature and art, forsaking all their pleasures like singing and dancing, and began to devote all their time and energy to making their state the finest fighting force in Greece.

Spartan soldiers fighting the Helots

A legendary figure—Lycurgus—is said to have been responsible for making the necessary changes in Sparta's way of life. He introduced a code of discipline which was iron-hard and which demanded unquestioning loyalty on the part of every Spartan. The army, and military training, became the most important things in Spartan life. Every man had to serve in the army and selection began at birth. Any child who appeared to be weak was taken from its parents and left on Mt Taygetus to die, or else was thrown from its steep sides. Only the strong survived.

Boys lived with their mothers until the age of seven when they were taken away and placed in special barracks. Grouped into small packs, led by older boys, they lived a hard life, under the careful supervision of a senior Spartan soldier. Everything was designed to make the boys tough, hardy and self-reliant. They always went barefoot, wearing heavy woollen clothes in summer and plain, thin tunics in winter. They slept on beds of reeds which they plucked from the river Eurotas. At night they had to go without torches to teach them to be unafraid of the dark. Their food was monotonous—a black, wheat porridge—and they were kept short, being forced to steal from neighbouring farms. Boys not caught stealing were admired for their initiative; those caught were beaten—not for dishonesty but for bad scouting. One boy, when caught red-handed in the theft of a tame fox, hid the animal in his cloak and allowed it to eat into his stomach, rather than confess the theft and so admit failure. Once a year a competition was held to see which boy could endure severe whip-lashing the longest. The packs frequently met in tough ball-games and in organized fights. They had practically no amusements and were discouraged from speaking more than was absolutely necessary. Their only songs were songs of war, such as those by Tyrtaeus, their national poet, calculated to inspire courage and absolute devotion to their native land. Here is a translation of part of a song:

> Let us battle for our country, giving up our breath,
> To save our darling children, never fearing death.
> Fight shield to shield, young soldiers, never turn to run
>   away,
> But steel your hearts with courage to enter in the fray.

The training of older boys was more directly related to army fighting, and two years were spent in the Crypteia, a sort of secret police. They spied on the Helots and killed in cold blood any who seemed too strong.

At the age of twenty, each young man was elected to be a member of a club or mess of about fifteen members. From then

Spartan boys training

They were taught not to be afraid of the dark

Each boy was whipped to see who could endure pain the longest

They were taught to steal without being caught *(above)*

Older boys in armour training to fight *(above right)*

Soldiers leaving for battle

on this would be his section in the army. He would live, eat and sleep there, even after marrying (which was not permitted until the age of thirty). In these clubs everything was shared, each member providing his share of the necessities such as food. The staple diet in the clubs consisted of barley-bread, figs, cheese and a kind of haggis. Such food was so uninviting that on one rare occasion when a foreigner was allowed to visit a club, he is supposed to have said: 'Now I know why the Spartans do not fear death!' Election to these clubs had to be unanimous. Not to be elected was a fate worse than death and fear of this must have given many boys the strength to complete the long, exhausting training.

Girls could not enlist in the army but they were keenly interested in it, and proud of its achievements and its efficiency. They too received athletic training just like the boys, in sports like running, discus-throwing and even wrestling. During this training, according to Plutarch, the girls wore so few clothes that most other Greeks were shocked. When the girls grew into women, their sole ambition was to produce strong sons who would become brave warriors. For women as well as for men, victory in battle was more important than personal survival. Every Spartan mother offered her son the same advice before he left for battle: 'Return carrying your shield, or carried on it'.

In addition to reorganizing the social system to combat the danger of Helot rebellion, Lycurgus also reshaped the government to make it more efficient and more representative of the people. He increased the number of men who could become full citizens (at the age of thirty) so as to enlarge the number of recruits to the army. He reduced the power of the kings and established a law that five Ephors (a word meaning 'overseers' or 'supervisors') should be appointed every year. They were elected by the people and all citizens were eligible to stand for this office. At first, their duties were to administer civil justice and to preside over the Apella. Soon, however, the Ephors, the representatives of the people, became the chief power in the state. They could even arrest or fine a king who did wrong. Once, as Plutarch tells us, they punished a king who had married a small woman, 'For she will bear us,' they said, 'not kings but kinglets.' The Ephors were also charged with seeing that the stern code of discipline devised by Lycurgus was adhered to by every Spartan.

The reforms of Lycurgus proved successful and provided Sparta with the finest army of the time. Never again did the Helots dare to stage a major uprising. The fame of the Spartan soldiers spread far beyond the boundaries of their city-state, and they became known throughout the ancient world for their skill, courage and self-discipline. Plutarch tells how, at one Olympic Games, an old man was unable to find a seat. Everyone ignored him until he reached the area where the Spartans were sitting. Every Spartan got up and offered him a seat. As he gratefully accepted, he said: 'All Greeks know what is right, but only Spartans do it.' In battle, the Spartans were incomparable. Even the bravest opponents felt some fear when they saw the Spartans, resplendent in their red cloaks, moving towards them in battle formation. Few Spartans were ever

Spartan soldiers in close battle formation

defeated. On the few occasions when defeat was inevitable, the Spartans never turned to run away. They always stood to the last, and fell fighting where they were. It was the Spartans'

Spartan soldiers in full armour

proud boast that all their soldiers' wounds were in front. To flee, to be wounded in the back was utter disgrace.

> And no man could count over and tell all the number of evils,
>   all that can come to a man, once he gives way to disgrace.
> For once a man reverses and runs in the terror of battle,
>   he offers his back, a tempting mark to spear from behind,
> and it is a shameful sight when a dead man lies in the dust there,
>   driven through from behind by the stroke of an enemy spear.
>   (*Tyrtaeus*)

The Spartans may have left no beautiful buildings or fine plays for us to remember and admire, but it was the courage of their soldiers, only three hundred in number, in resisting the might of Persia at Thermopylae in 480 BC and so delaying the Persian advance, that saved Greece from defeat and enslavement. These three hundred and the city which produced them are not forgotten.

Things to do:

Section A

1 Write down as your heading *Sparta*. Underline. Now write out these sentences filling in the blank spaces:
   (a) Everything in Sparta was geared for one thing—.......
   (b) The early Spartans had come from .... and settled in ....
   (c) These Spartans conquered ....
   (d) The Perioikoi were ....
   (e) The Helots were ....
   (f) The Spartans always feared that ....
   (g) In 650 BC the Helots .... After this the Spartans realized that .... They turned their backs on .... and began to devote all their time to ....

2 This time your heading is *Spartan Life*. Now answer the following questions:
   (a) You are a Spartan boy aged thirteen. Describe the life that you have had so far and the life that still awaits you. You should include as many accurate facts as you can, including details about selection, training, exercises, family-life, food, soldier's life, dangers of life and so on. Draw and colour some pictures to illustrate your answer.

(b) What sort of life did Spartan women have? Write a short paragraph to describe their life.

3 Your final heading is *Spartan Government*. Answer these questions:

(a) How many kings did Sparta have? What were their main duties?

(b) Explain as briefly as you can: Gerousia; Apella; Ephors.

Section B

1 From a dictionary find out the meaning of (a) 'spartan'; (b) 'laconic'. How are the modern meanings of these words connected with the Ancient Spartans?

2 Draw a picture of a Spartan soldier on to cardboard. Paint your drawing. Now cut round the outline and fix a strong piece of card to the back as a stand. Perhaps you and your friends could make a squadron of soldiers.

3 On strong paper draw a circle the size of a shield. Draw a design on the circle which could have appeared on a Spartan shield. The design should be fierce enough to scare the enemy! Paint the shield and display it on the wall.

4 The songs of Tyrtaeus were meant to inspire Spartan soldiers to bravery. Compose a song to have such an effect on the soldiers of your country.

7 Athenian Democracy

Pericles

Amongst the ideals which the Greeks prized were a respect for law and order and a love of freedom. One of the most famous Athenian statesmen, Pericles, said on one occasion:

> Each single one of our citizens . . . is able to show himself the rightful owner of his own person

and

> We are free and tolerant in our private lives, but in public affairs we keep to the law. . . . We give our obedience to those whom we put in positions of authority, and we obey the laws themselves.

This is the kind of thinking which gave rise to what we now know as 'democracy', a word which has come to us from two Greek words δημος 'the people' and κρατος 'power' or 'rule'. So democracy really means 'power to the people'. And that was exactly what Pericles meant when he described the Athenian form of government as follows—

> Our constitution is called a democracy because power is in the hands not of a minority but of the whole people.

As we have already seen in Chapter 1 Ancient Greece was not one large country with one government. It was divided up into many small independent states, each centred around a city, and each with its own form of government. A look at a map of Greece will help you to find the reason for this; Greece is a very mountainous country, and is cut into by many inlets of the sea. And so it became easy for a small city-state to spring up in these regions which were separated from the rest of the country by mountains and sea. The Greek name for such a state is πολις, a word which has given us our English words like politics, politician, etc.

You can see some of these Greek city-states on the map opposite.

The city-states of Greece

Athens came to be famous as a 'democracy', but it had not always had that form of government. In its early days it had been ruled by kings and tyrants (or dictators). But the last of these tyrants was driven out by the nobles around 510 BC, and it was one of these nobles—Cleisthenes—who reformed the government of Athens on democratic lines.

Cleisthenes divided Attica into ten blocks which they called 'tribes'. Each of the ten tribes elected fifty representatives above thirty years old to be members of the Boule, whose duty it was to carry out the daily work of government. They received payment for their work, and their main duties were to make proposals for the Ecclesia (assembly of citizens) to discuss, and to ensure that decisions of the assembly were put into practice. The representatives of each of the ten tribes took it in turn to be in charge of the Boule for one-tenth of the year each.

The Ecclesia was the main source of power: it was the body which made the final decisions by which Athens was governed. Every male citizen of Athens over eighteen years old was a member. It met forty times a year on a sloping hillside, the Pnyx, near the Acropolis, where there was rock platform known as the Bema. Citizens who were rather late in leaving the market-place to attend the Ecclesia were rounded up by a cord

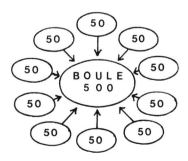

that had been soaked in red dye: any whose clothes were stained with the dye were liable to a fine. Citizens sat down facing the platform—usually there were between 5000 and 6000 of them—and the proceedings opened with prayers and the sacrifice of a black pig. The proposals put forward by the Boule were read out, and the discussions were then open to any citizen; while speaking a citizen stood on the Bema, and wore a crown on his head.

Orator addressing the Ecclesia

An ostrakon

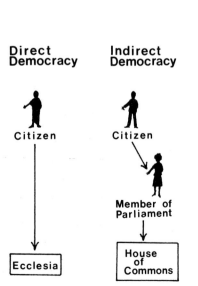

Direct Democracy

Indirect Democracy

Citizen

Citizen

Member of Parliament

Ecclesia

House of Commons

After discussion a vote was taken by a show of hands, and so a law was made. In cases where they were voting for the banishment of a citizen, the people voted by placing in large containers small fragments of pottery—the Greeks called such a fragment an Ostrakon—on which they had written the name of the person they wished to banish. This kind of banishment has come to be called ostracism, and today we still talk about ostracizing a person.

So every citizen of Athens had a direct say in the government of his city (direct democracy); government by elected representatives like our Members of Parliament was unknown (indirect democracy).

The kind of democracy that ancient Athens had could operate only when the population was fairly small and when citizens were willing to be involved in governing their city. So Pericles could say:

Here each individual is interested not only in his own affairs but in the affairs of the state as well—even those who are mostly occupied with their own business are extremely well-informed on general politics . . . we do not say that a man who takes no interest in politics is a man who minds his own business; we say that he has no business here at all.

Also citizens had to have time to devote to politics, and this was made possible by the fact that there were plenty of slaves in Athens to do the work and leave their masters free to attend the Assembly and take on public duties.

It should be remembered, however, that Athenian democracy was rather restricted. In fact it was not every male over eighteen years of age who lived in Athens who was a member of the Ecclesia, but every male citizen of Athens, i.e. who had himself been born in Athens and whose parents had also been born in Athens. This was another factor in making Athenian democracy work.

In Athens there were several public posts held by various officials; the highest ranking of these were ten generals, called Strategoi, one from each tribe, who took it in turn to be in command and who held office for only one year. Most of the officials were chosen by lot as this meant that everyone had the chance to hold office whether rich or poor. But there was one difficulty: a weak inefficient man might be chosen. To prevent this the Strategoi were elected by the people. The main duties of the Strategoi were to be in charge of the finance of the city, to be in charge of the army and fortifications, to lead the army in war, and to be the official representatives of the state. The Strategoi were assisted in carrying out their duties by nine Archons. It was usually the Archons who presided over the law-courts. Another of Cleisthenes' provisions was that public officials, except the Strategoi, should be paid for their services to the state; this meant that even poorer men could afford to hold office.

We have mentioned Pericles and quoted some of his famous statements about democracy. He managed to have himself re-elected Strategos fifteen times: he sincerely believed in the democratic form of government and wanted to make Athens a great city. So he encouraged the Athenians to build beautiful buildings like the Parthenon to adorn their city and to expand the influence of Athens all over the Greek world.

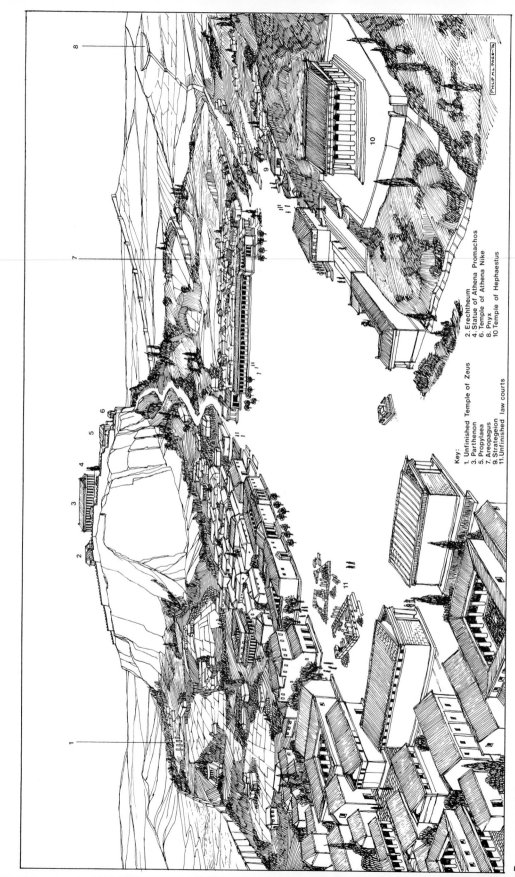

Key:
1. Unfinished Temple of Zeus
2. Erechtheum
3. Parthenon
4. Statue of Athena Promachos
5. Propylaea
6. Temple of Athena Nike
7. Areopagus
8. Pnyx
9. Strategeion
10. Temple of Hephaestus
11. Unfinished law courts

PHILIP M. PAGE '76

Panorama of Athens

Things to do:

Section A

1 Write the heading *Athenian Democracy*. Answer the following questions:
  (a) What does the word 'democracy' really mean?
  (b) Write down the two Greek words (with meanings) from which it comes.
  (c) Copy out the explanation of democracy which Pericles gave.

2 How was Athens governed before it was a democracy? What is the name of the person who introduced the new democratic form of government?

3 Write the heading *The Boule*. Complete these sentences:
  (a) The members of the Boule were ....
  (b) Their main duty was ....
  (c) They did this by .... and ....
  (d) Copy the diagram on page 43 to show how the Boule was formed.

4 Write the heading *The Ecclesia*. Answer these questions:
  (a) Who were the members of the Ecclesia?
  (b) How often did it meet?
  (c) Where did it meet?
  (d) Who were allowed to speak in the Ecclesia?

5 Copy the diagram on page 44. Give some reasons why it was possible for direct democracy to work in Athens but not in Britain today.

6 Write the heading *Government Officials*. Answer these questions.
  (a) Who were the Strategoi, and what does their name really mean?
  (b) How long did they hold power?
  (c) What were their main duties?
  (d) Who were the Archons, and what did they do?
  (e) Why was it important that public officials should be paid?

Section B

1 This chapter has suggested some advantages in the Athenian form of democracy. It also had disadvantages. Can you suggest some?

2 Draw a picture of a speaker addressing the Ecclesia.

3 The Ecclesia could banish a person for ten years. Choose a person you would like to see banished and write a speech to be delivered in the Ecclesia asking for his banishment and exile.

8 The Persian Wars

The fight for freedom

The Persian Empire was so vast that it would take an army three months to march from the Aegean Sea to its capital, Susa. Over this mighty empire King Darius ruled. Although he was a just ruler he expected his subjects to obey all his commands without question and even the greatest Persian nobles fell on their faces when they came before him. The Greeks loved freedom and hated the idea of being ruled by the wishes of one man. When Darius tried to compel Greeks to obey his orders, it is not at all surprising that this resulted in bitter warfare between the Greeks and the Persians.

Greek city-states around 500 BC

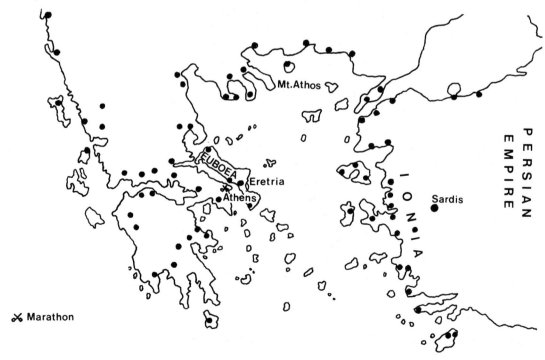

King Darius

The first Greeks to come into conflict with the Persian Empire were the Ionians, who had built their colonies on the west coast of Asia Minor. As it expanded westwards the Persian Empire took over their towns. They were forced to accept a Persian overlord, pay a special tax to the Persians, and they were also liable to special military service. For a time the Ionians submitted to this treatment but at last a rebellion broke out in Miletus, the leading city of the Ionians. They asked Athens and Sparta to help them to free themselves from the yoke of the Persians. Athens sent twenty ships and Eretria on the island of Euboea sent five. They joined the Ionians and marched against the city of Sardis, burning it to the ground.

Herodotus, the Greek historian, describes the effect which the news had on King Darius.

The story goes that when Darius learnt of the disaster, he did not give a thought to the Ionians, knowing perfectly well that the punishment for their revolt would come; instead the first thing he did was to ask who the Athenians were, and then, on being told, gave orders that his bow should be handed to him. He took the bow, set an arrow on the string, shot it up into the air, and cried: 'Grant, O God, that I may punish the Athenians.' Then he commanded one of his servants to repeat to him the words, 'Master, remember the Athenians', three times, whenever he sat down to dinner.

The invasion of Darius

The Ionians were soon defeated in a sea battle, Miletus was

recaptured and the Greeks in Ionia were punished most severely. Now Darius resolved to conquer Greece. The first fleet that he sent was wrecked by a storm off Mount Athos. But in 490 BC he sent another fleet carrying a strong army which had special orders to capture Eretria and Athens.

Eretria was captured and the people were carried off into slavery. The Persians now landed at Marathon, twenty-six miles north of Athens. The Athenians sent Pheidippides, a swift runner, to Sparta to call for help.

'Men of Sparta', the message ran, 'the Athenians ask you to help them, and not to stand by while the most ancient city of Greece is crushed and enslaved by a foreign invader. Already Eretria is destroyed, and her people in chains, and Greece is the weaker by the loss of one fine city.'

The Spartans, however, declared that they could not send help until the moon was full as they were celebrating a religious festival.

Athens was in great danger. If they delayed, the city would be attacked. The Athenians marched out to meet the Persians at Marathon accompanied only by 1000 men from the little city of Plataea, and lined up on the hills overlooking the sea. The Greeks relied mostly on heavily armed foot-soldiers called hoplites, who stood shoulder to shoulder holding their shields in front of them and with their heavy spears thrust forward. The Persians were greatly superior in numbers and had a great many horsemen and archers, but their soldiers were not as heavily armed as the Greek soldiers.

For several days the armies faced each other. Some of the Athenian commanders did not wish to risk a battle. But one general, Miltiades, persuaded them to fight. He ordered the hoplites to lengthen their line until it was as long as that of the Persians; the two wings were strong but the line in the centre was only a few ranks deep. Then the Athenians advanced at a run towards the enemy who were about a mile away. There was a terrible struggle. The Persians broke through the Greek centre, and forced them back towards the hills. But the Athenians on one wing and the Plataeans on the other were both victorious, put their opponents to flight and closed in round the Persians who had broken through the centre. Here too they were victorious. The Persians were routed and fled to their ships. 6400 Persians lay dead on the field of Marathon. Only 192 Athenians had fallen.

A famous story is told of how the news of victory was carried to Athens. A runner (some say he was the same Pheidippides who had run to Sparta for help), had only the strength to gasp 'Rejoice, we have conquered', before he

Greek Hoplite

collapsed and died of exhaustion. In memory of this the long-distance race known as the 'Marathon' was named.

Miltiades immediately marched his troops back to Athens. He knew that the Persian fleet would try to reach the city. The Athenians arrived back in time. The Persian commanders decided not to risk another battle and sailed off to Asia. For the moment the Athenians had saved Greece.

Athenian burial mound, Marathon

The youth of Marathon

The second invasion

Darius was furious when he heard the news of Marathon. He decided to lead a much larger army against Greece, but died before he could do so. In 480 BC his son Xerxes was ready to invade Greece with a huge army. Herodotus tells us:

> There was not a nation in all Asia that he did not take with him against Greece; save for the great rivers there was not a stream his army drank from that was not drunk dry.

Xerxes' preparations for the invasion included the building

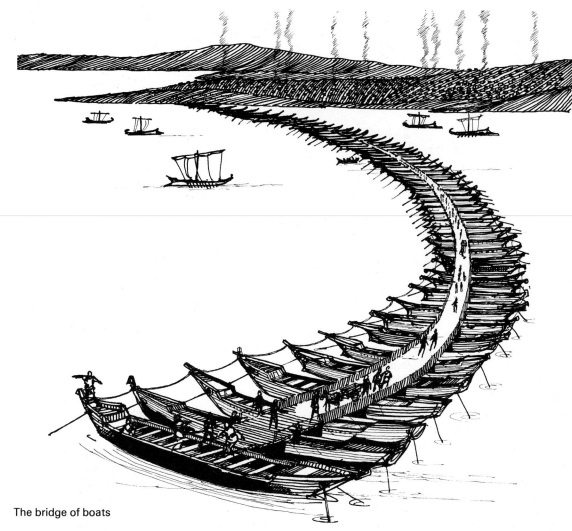

The bridge of boats

of a bridge a mile and a half long over the Hellespont, made by joining together boats anchored side by side and building a road over them. He also had dumps of food made along his route to supplement the diet of his massive army, and a canal cut so that the great fleet which would sail along the coast keeping pace with the army would not have to sail round the headland of Mount Athos where Darius lost his fleet in his first attempt to attack Greece.

For seven days and seven nights the Great King watched his men cross the bridge into Europe. On they marched through Thrace and Macedonia moving southwards until they came to a place called Thermopylae, a narrow pass between the mountains and the sea, which has been called the Gateway of Greece.

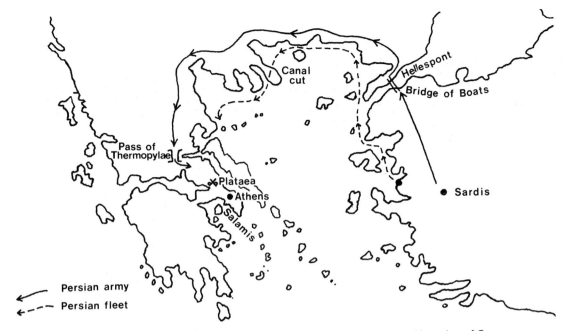

To Xerxes' surprise he found the pass blocked by the Spartan king Leonidas with 300 Spartans and some troops from other Greek cities. The Spartans were in front of the Greek line—so Xerxes' spies reported—and they seemed unconcerned. They were busy doing gymnastics and combing their long hair as they always did before battle. The Athenian fleet meanwhile were ready to engage the Persian ships at Artemisium so that the Persian fleet would either have to sail round Euboea or to attack the Greek ships in the narrow waters near Thermopylae, where the Greeks would find it easier to fight them.

Knowing what a small army was in front of him, Xerxes hurled masses of his soldiers against the defenders of the narrow pass. But every Persian attack was hurled back again with heavy losses. Eventually Xerxes sent in his best troops, the 'King's Immortals', expecting that they would finish off the Spartans. They were no more successful than the rest had been. Xerxes, watching the battle from where he sat, is said to have leapt to his feet three times in terror for his army. Next day the attack was renewed but with no more success. Xerxes was baffled.

Then Leonidas was betrayed. There was a track through the mountains. A Greek called Ephialtes who knew of it came to Xerxes and for a great sum of money offered to show the Persians the path. A strong force was sent through the mountains to the rear of the Greeks. When news of this reached Leonidas he sent most of his men back to safety. He himself

King Xerxes

53

with all his Spartans and with 700 men from Thespiae resolved to stay where they were and to face death bravely. Herodotus describes the battle.

As the Persian army advanced to the assault the Greeks under Leonidas, knowing that the fight would be their last, pressed forward into the wider part of the pass much further than they had done before: in the previous days' fighting they had been holding the wall and making sorties from behind it into the narrow neck, but now they left the confined space and battle was joined on more open ground. Many of the invaders fell; behind them the company commanders plied their whips, driving the men remorselessly on. Many fell into the sea and were drowned, and still more were trampled to death by their friends. No one could count the number of the dead. The Greeks, who knew that the enemy were on their way round by the mountain track and that death was inevitable, fought with reckless desperation, exerting every ounce of strength that was in them against the invader. By this time most of their spears were broken, and they were killing Persians with their swords.

In the course of the fight Leonidas fell, having fought like a man indeed. Many distinguished Spartans were killed at his side—their names, like the names of all the 300, I have made myself acquainted with, because they deserve to be remembered. Among the Persian dead too, were many men of high distinction—for instance, two brothers of Xerxes.

There was a bitter struggle over the body of Leonidas; four times the Greeks drove the enemy off, and at last by their valour succeeded in dragging it away. So it went on until the fresh troops with Ephialtes were close at hand; and then, when the Greeks knew that they had come, the character of the fighting changed. They withdrew into the narrow neck of the pass, behind the walls, and took up position in a single compact body on the little hill at the entrance to the pass, where the stone lion in memory of Leonidas stands today. Here they resisted to the last, with their swords, if they had them, and, if not, with their hands and teeth, until the Persians, coming on from the front over the ruins of the wall and closing in from behind, finally overwhelmed them.

Years later the grateful Greeks erected a stone over the graves of these Spartans. On it was inscribed:

Go tell the Spartans, you who read:
We took their orders, and are dead.

Thermopylae had merely delayed the Persians. Now the

whole of Greece was in danger. Anxiously the Athenians consulted the oracle of Apollo at Delphi. (There was at Delphi a temple where the priestess of Apollo would tell those who asked her what the will of the gods was.) The answer from the priestess was:

> The wooden wall only shall not fall, but help you and your
> children.
> But await not the host of horse and foot coming from Asia,
> Nor be still but turn your back and withdraw from the foe.

This answer led to much discussion. What did the 'wooden wall' mean? Some felt sure it meant they should build a wooden fence round the city. But Themistocles, the Athenian leader, thought it meant that they should abandon the city and take to their wooden ships. The Athenians were persuaded to leave their homes. The women and children were taken to the islands of Salamis and Aegina. The men took to the ships. When Xerxes reached Athens he found it almost deserted. He seized the city, burned down the temples and houses, and sent a messenger triumphantly back to his capital Susa to tell them that the burning of Sardis was avenged.

The Athenian fleet of triremes, together with ships from other Greek cities, were gathered near the island of Salamis. The Peloponnesian generals wanted to retreat to the Isthmus of Corinth and to abandon everything except the Peloponnesus to the Persians. Themistocles, however, urged them to stay and face the Persians in the narrow waters round Salamis. He realized that the Greek triremes, although outnumbered greatly (there were only 380 Greek triremes to face the 1000 ships which Xerxes still had left), would have an advantage fighting in a confined space and in seas which they knew so well. The Greek triremes had reinforced prows which would ram the side of enemy ships and hole them. They were also very manœuvrable and could be turned quickly by skilled oarsmen.

Before the Spartans and their Peloponnesian allies could get a chance to leave with their ships, Themistocles sent a messenger to Xerxes pretending to be a traitor and telling him that the Greeks were intending to escape that night. The Persians believed this and decided to block the channels with their ships to prevent the Greek fleet from escaping. They sailed up and down all night and none of the men had time for sleep.

In the morning while Xerxes sat on a golden throne over-looking Salamis, the Persian ships sailed in to finish off the Greeks. As the Persian ships advanced, the Greeks backed away, luring them further into the narrows. When the Persians

Themistocles

Triremes

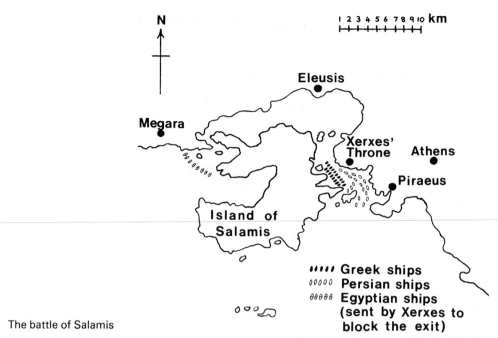

The battle of Salamis

Salamis today

were packed close together, the Greek triremes charged. What the effect was we can imagine from the description given by the Greek writer Aeschylus in his play 'The Persians'. A messenger tells Xerxes' mother of the battle.

> Soon in that narrow space
> Our ships were jammed in hundreds; none could help
> another.

They rammed each other with their prows of bronze and
   some
Were stripped of every oar. Meanwhile the enemy
Came round us in a ring and charged. Our vessels heeled
Over; the sea was hidden, carpeted with wrecks
And dead men; all the shores and reefs were full of dead.
Then every ship we had broke rank and rowed for life.
The whole sea was one din of shrieks and dying groans,
Till night and darkness hid the scene. If I should speak
For ten days and ten nights, I could not tell you all
That day's agony. But know this: never before
In one day died so vast a company of men.

Xerxes watching the battle

Salamis had saved the freedom of the Greeks. Xerxes
retreated back to Asia. He left an army behind with the Persian
general, Mardonius, but this army too was beaten by the
Greeks at Plataea in the following year.

Greece had defended her liberty and had beaten back the
cruel invader who had tried to enslave her. This was one of the
great moments in history. Many years later, in the nineteenth
century, when Greece once more fought for her freedom, this
time against the Ottoman Empire, the English poet Lord Byron
looked forward with hope as he recalled the Greeks of 490 BC
and their determination to remain free.

The mountains look on Marathon—
And Marathon looks on the sea;
And musing there an hour alone,
I dream'd that Greece might still be free;
For standing on the Persians' grave,
I could not deem myself a slave.

57

Things to do:

Write down the heading *The Persian Wars*. Underline it.

Section A

1 Complete the following paragraphs:

When the cities of Ionia rose in revolt against King . . . . of . . . ., the Greek cities of . . . . . . and Eretria sent help. They burned the city of . . . . King . . . . was very angry and vowed to punish the Greeks. He sent an army into Greece, but it was defeated at . . . . . . by the Greek army which consisted mostly of Athenians. The . . . . could not help them as they were busy with a religious festival.

Ten years later, King . . . . the son of King . . . . was ready to avenge the defeat of his father's army. He led a vast army into Europe, crossing the . . . . by means of a bridge of . . . . The Greeks attempted to stop his advance at . . . ., a narrow pass between the . . . . and the . . . . But even the courage of the . . . . led by their king, Leonidas, could not stop the Persians. They marched on to . . . . . . and burned the city. Earlier the . . . . had taken their women and children to a safe place and had taken to the ships. The Greek fleet anchored between the small island of . . . . and the mainland. . . . ., the Athenian general, tricked the Persians into sending their ships to attack the Greek ships in the narrow straits where they could not make use of their great number. As a result the Persians were totally defeated. King . . . . fled back home, and the army he left behind was defeated the following year at . . . .

Section B

1 How long is a Marathon race today? Explain how it got its name.
2 Imagine that you are one of the 300 Spartans at Thermopylae staying behind with Leonidas. Write a final entry in your personal diary as you wait for the Persians to attack.
3 Draw a Greek trireme. Colour it.
4 Herodotus, the Greek historian, wrote:
   A man of Trachis told a Spartan that when the Persians shot their arrows there would be so many of them that they would hide the sun. 'That is good news,' replied the Spartan, 'for if the Persians hide the sun, then we will be able to fight in the shade.'

Write a sentence telling what you think this story tells us about the Spartans.

5 Draw and colour a picture of Xerxes army crossing the Hellespont.

6 Using a full page of your jotter compose the front page of a newspaper carrying a report of the Greek victory at Salamis. It should include a prominent heading and a picture as well as the report.

9 Greek Architecture

Royal Scottish Gallery, Edinburgh

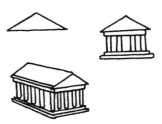

Stirling's Library, Glasgow

Today, in many cities and towns throughout the world, you can see buildings like those in the picture on the left. The design of these buildings can be traced back through history to the days of Ancient Greece, over two thousand years ago.

The Greeks were expert builders. They designed and produced structures of outstanding beauty and form. The style of building most favoured is as distinctive as the land of Greece itself, and has survived the test of time to the present day. It is basically very simple—a sloping roof supported on all sides by pillars or columns, and usually rectangular in shape.

Using this simple design and paying close attention to detail, form and proportion, the Greeks constructed buildings which were (and still are) admired and copied the whole world over.

The most remarkable of these Greek buildings were those erected in honour of their gods—divine beings like Zeus and Athena, Poseidon and Apollo. Many of these buildings, or temples as they are called, are still standing today and provide a lasting tribute to the skill of the Greek architects and builders. A temple was normally built in a sacred grove which was surrounded by a wall. The worshippers would enter through a covered gateway into the sanctuary where the temple stood.

At first, these temples were made of wood, but the Greeks soon realized that wood was not the best material for building—it was not very strong, it could rot easily and it often caught fire.

59

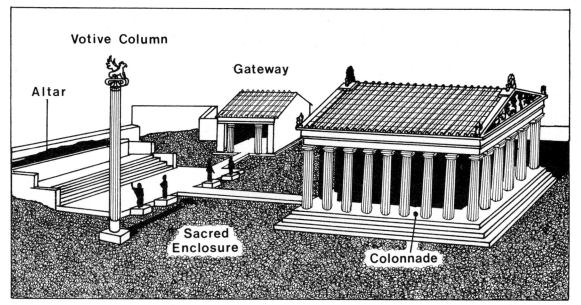

Votive Column

Gateway

Altar

Sacred Enclosure

Colonnade

A Greek temple and its sanctuary

For a replacement they turned to stone—much stronger and more durable than wood. The people of Athens were especially fortunate as they had, near to where they lived, large quantities of marble—a material admirably suited for building. It was soon discovered that stone had yet another advantage over wood—it could be carved and shaped for decoration without weakening. There was no reason to leave the columns plain and unadorned as the old wooden ones had been, and so various designs for the columns developed. There were three important ones.

The simplest of these designs is the Doric, developed by the Greeks of Dorian descent. The Doric column is really quite plain and has no base.

The capital, or stone cushion at the top of the column used to spread the weight evenly, is a simple square piece of stone. Each column is usually fluted or carved with twenty vertical grooves to give a light-shade effect.

Men fluting a column

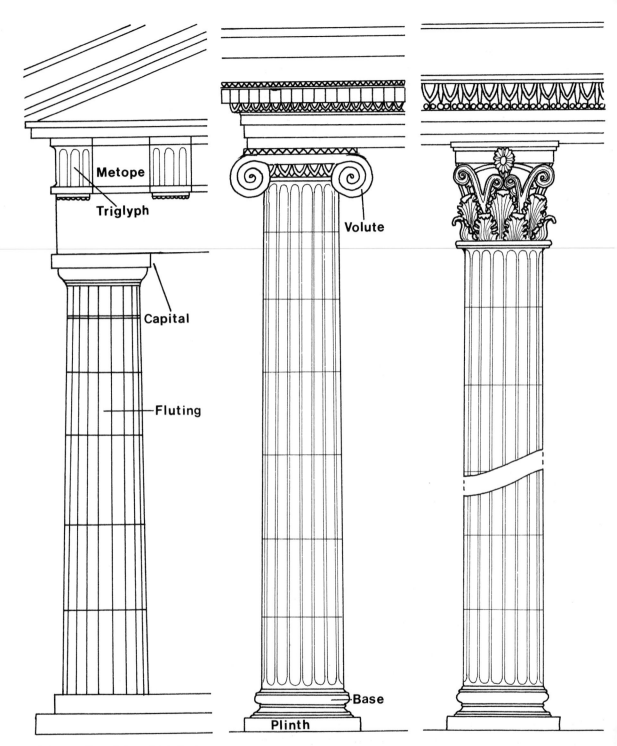

Metope

Triglyph

Capital

Fluting

Volute

Base

Plinth

Columns. From left to right: Doric,
Ionic, Corinthian

The other commonly used design was developed by the Greeks of Ionian descent, especially those who had colonized the coast of Asia Minor (modern Turkey) and the adjoining islands. This type of column is therefore called Ionic. It is slimmer than the Doric column and has a proper base. It has finer fluting than the Doric but perhaps the most striking difference is seen in the capital. In stark contrast to the plain square stone of the Doric, the Ionic capital has an intricate, curling design, resembling a scroll. This scroll-like design is called a volute.

One ancient expert on architecture, Vitruvius, when comparing the Doric and Ionic columns, suggested that the sturdy Doric column was based on a man's figure, while the slender Ionic more closely resembled that of a young woman.

A variation of the Ionic order is the Corinthian. The capital of this style is carved in the likeness of acanthus leaves. (The acanthus is a kind of thistle found in Greece.) The Greeks used this style sparingly, but it later became a favourite with the Romans who copied much of Greek architecture.

Design and decoration were not limited to the column-shaft and the capital. Just below the roof, on temples of Doric design, were small, square pieces of stone, delicately carved with scenes from history and legend. These are called metopes. Interspersed with the metopes were other squares with a much plainer design, often just three vertical grooves. These squares are called triglyphs. The word 'frieze' is often used to describe such decorations placed on temples at this point.

The Ionic and Corinthian styles no longer used triglyphs and metopes. Instead, the frieze became one continuous piece of sculpture. The large, triangular areas at each end of the temple were also used for decoration.

A Greek temple. The triangular area is called the pediment

This area, known as the pediment, often contained scenes from mythology, beautifully carved on the stone. All these carvings were vividly painted in bright, life-like colours.

Temples and other buildings, constructed along these lines,

63

graced the whole of the Greek world, but nowhere could they be seen to better advantage than in the city of Athens. Now the capital of Greece, and in ancient times one of the most important cities in the world, Athens had been ravaged by the Persians in 480 BC. They had entered the city and set fire to it. Even the temples of the gods, built on the sacred ground of the Acropolis, the high, rocky crag in the centre of the city, were burned, including a new one, only half-built, in honour of Athena, the patron goddess of the city.

After the Persians had later been defeated, Athens became the leading city in the Greek world. Pericles, the most powerful statesman of the time, decided that Athens should be the most beautiful city in Greece. As a beginning, he laid plans for the building of new temples on the Acropolis—including the Parthenon, in honour of Athena, perhaps the most beautiful of all Greek buildings. The complex of buildings on the Acropolis, begun by Pericles in 447 BC, was not finished until 407 BC, some twenty-two years after Pericles' death. On completion, it must have looked something like this:

The Acropolis in ancient times

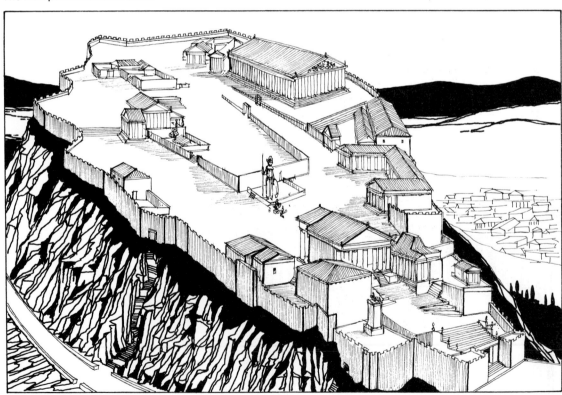

Let us imagine that you or someone in your class could go back in time to view the Acropolis in all its glory. The year is 400 BC. Athens has just fought a long war against Sparta and lost. She has fallen from power, but still remains the centre of Greek civilization and culture. Your guide on the tour of the Acropolis is Nikos, a young Athenian.

— Hello! Welcome to our city! I'm glad you've arrived safely.
— Hello, Nikos, it's nice to be here. I'm really looking forward to seeing round your city. I've heard so much about it, especially about the famous buildings on the Acropolis. How impressive they look; they stand so high above the city, glistening in the sun. You must be able to see them for miles.
— Yes, you certainly can. Our Athenian sailors are always glad when they see the helmet of Athena Promachos gleaming in the sun. Then they know they are home, though they may still be far out at sea.
— Athena what?
— Come on! Let's go up to the Acropolis. I'll explain everything when we get there. Let's save our breath for a moment.

A short time later our two friends have arrived at the entrance to the complex. Our time-traveller speaks first.

— Phew! What a steep climb!
— Nearly there! We're coming up to the Propylaea. The whole of the Acropolis is sacred to our gods—a sort of holy place or sanctuary. The Propylaea is the gateway through which all worshippers enter the sanctuary.
— Why is there a gap in the steps here, Nikos?

The Propylaea

— The builders left that space so that the animals which are taken up to the temples for sacrifice could pass through easily. They might have stumbled over steps and that would be a bad omen.

— I see. I must say, these pillars are really huge.

— Yes, they're the biggest, thickest type of pillar we use. They are called Doric. They're quite plain but despite that most people find them impressive.

— I certainly do!

— We're now passing through the Propylaea. Do you see any difference in the columns now?

— Yes, they're thinner and they've got some kind of decoration at the top. It's almost like a scroll or a ram's horn.

— That's right. Quite a good description. We call this type of column Ionic. It's much more graceful than the Doric, don't you agree?

— Well, I suppose so. But it's probably not quite so impressive —at least that's what I think.

— Ah, I know exactly what you mean. I suppose it's all a matter of taste.

They pass through the gateway and enter the sanctuary itself. The first thing they see is a huge statue, over fifty feet high. Our time-traveller gasps at the size.

— Wow! What a size! Who is it supposed to be?

— That's the statue I mentioned earlier, remember? Our sailors can see it far out at sea.

— Oh yes, I remember. It's a statue of Athena Pro . . .
Prom . . . em . . .
— Athena Promachos. That means Athena the Champion.
We call her that because she is our patron goddess, the
defender of our city. The statue was designed by Pheidias.
Do you know what it's made from?
— Looks like some kind of metal.
— Yes, it's bronze. It was cast from enemy weapons and
armour captured at the battle of Salamis when we defeated
the Persians.
— It's quite magnificent.

He stands gazing up at the face of the statue.

— Come on! Let's go over this way and see the biggest
building on the Acropolis.
— It certainly is big. It must cover an area as large as a football
pitch.
— What?
— Oh nothing. I was just commenting on the size of the
temple. What's it called?
— It's the Parthenon. It is dedicated to Athena. She is often
called the maiden goddess and in our language the word
for maiden is Parthenos. Hence the name. Do you remember
the name for plain columns like these?
— I think so, em . . . Doric!
— Good! The columns here are very tall as you can see. They
must be about six times the height of a man, don't you
think?
— At least that.
— If you look closely, you'll see that the columns are not whole
pieces of marble. They are made from small drums of

A drum from a column

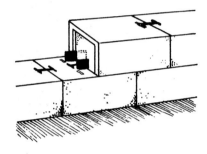

Metal clamps holding blocks together

The steps were curved to make them seem level

marble, one placed on top of the other. There are usually about ten in a column.

— Did they use mortar or cement to hold them in place?

— No. Each drum has a hole in the top. A piece of wood is fitted in there so as to stick out and fit into a hole in the next drum and so on. It's the same with the walls—no cement there either, but sometimes small metal clamps and dowels were used to hold the stones in position.

— Amazing! Everything fits together so well. You couldn't even push a needle through those joints!

— Our builders are clever men. We are very proud of them. Here! If I place this little stone at this end of the steps and you go to the other end and look along, do you think you'll see the stone?

— Of course! The steps are so flat and level.

— Try it.

— O.K.

— Get well down! your eye level with the step! Well, can you see it?

— No, I can't. It's incredible! The steps seem so level; yet, if I can't see the stone, they can't be, can they?

— You're right. The architects who designed the Parthenon, Ictinus and Callicrates, realized that if they made the steps dead level they would seem to sag in the middle. So, to avoid this, they made them rise a little in the middle before falling again—a sort of gentle curve. Clever, eh?

— Yes, it is. You'd never know just to look. Can we go inside the temple now?
— No, I'm afraid not. Only the priests are allowed inside. All worshippers of the goddess stand outside.
— What's inside?
— If we go up to the door there we may be able to see in. There, do you see? The most beautiful statue ever—of of our beloved goddess Athena.
— Who made this statue?
— Pheidias again. The statue is made of wood, plated with gold for the dress and ivory for the skin. It's only a little smaller than the other statue but it's much more beautiful. Every four years the people of Athens honour Athena by making a new robe to drape over the statue. A great procession winds its way through the streets of the city up to the Acropolis. The robe is stretched out for all to see on the mast of a ship which is dragged along on rollers. We call this the Panathenaic festival.
— It must be quite a sight. I wish I could see it.
— I'm afraid you can't—it's not held this year. But I can show you the next best thing. Let's go up the steps and through the columns. There! Do you see those carvings up there? That is the frieze and it shows the Panathenaic festival. The entire procession has been carved on marble— horsemen, chariots, elders, musicians, girls pouring libations, animals for sacrifice, magistrates, priests. It's all there, just as if the procession was actually moving round the temple till they meet here above the entrance.

They both walk round examining the frieze in detail until they arrive back at the entrance.

— I've never seen anything like it, Nikos. The figures are so life-like; they really seem to be moving. Are there any more sculptures like that?
— Yes. Come on. I'll show you. Down the steps. There! Look up at the top part of the temple. Do you see the large triangular area? That's called the pediment. The sculptures in that one above the door represent the birth of Athena herself. The one at the other end shows the contest between Athena and Poseidon. Do you know the story?
— No, I don't think so.
— Athena and Poseidon had a contest to see who should be patron of the city. Both offered the people a gift. Poseidon struck the rock with his trident and produced a salt-spring. Athena made an olive tree grow. The people

Statue of Athena

Peristyle—part of the covered walk-way around the Parthenon

Pediment sculpture

Metope, showing Centaur fighting Lapith

preferred Athena's gift and so she was the winner. That's why the city is called after her—Athens means Athena's city.

— That's an interesting story and I remember my teacher saying that the olive is one of the main crops of Greece.

— Yes, it is very important to us. Now, do you see those smaller sculptures below the pediment—the little squares? They are called metopes and show scenes from battles—gods against giants, Greeks against Trojans, centaurs against Lapiths.

— Centaurs? What are they?

— They were half-horse and half-man. When they were invited to a wedding feast by the Lapiths, a tribe living nearby, they disgraced themselves by first getting drunk and then trying to run off with the bride. Needless to say, a fierce battle followed.

— I do like the colours they've used on the sculptures. They're so bright and life-like. Do you mind if I take a closer look?

— No, not at all. I'll wait here for you.

A few minutes later they are together again.

— It's almost time to go now, but there's one last thing I want to show you. It's a small temple called the Erechtheum and it's quite unusual. It's built where the contest between Athena and Poseidon took place. You can still see the olive

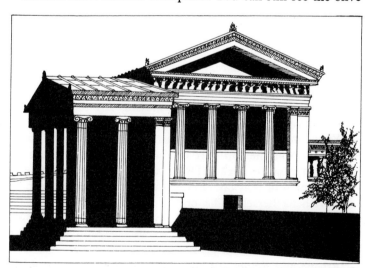

The Erechtheum

tree. It was burned by the Persians but new shoots sprang up to give us fresh hope. We're getting closer; do you notice anything unusual now?

The Caryatids

— Yes, there! They've used women instead of columns to support the roof.
— Well, statues of women—not the real thing! They are called Caryatids. This part of the temple, not surprisingly, is named 'The Porch of the Maidens'. Do you see anything else unusual?
— No. I don't think so.
— Well, the temple is built on three different levels. Where we are now, at the Porch of the Maidens, is on the highest level.
— The builders have done a good job—the whole temple seems quite in one piece, despite the different levels. But wouldn't it have been easier to level the ground.
— Impossible. Remember that this is sacred ground. It would have been improper to tamper with it in that way.
— I understand.
— It's getting late now. We must go back down to the city.

I hope you've enjoyed your visit to the Acropolis. Perhaps you can understand now why we in Athens are so proud of our buildings.

— Yes, I can well understand why. I've never seen such magnificent buildings before. The Parthenon is especially beautiful. So graceful and elegant. I could never forget it.

Our time-traveller turns to have one last look as the sun begins to set, bathing the temple in a glow of rose-light. His visit is over. He must return to his own time.

If our time-traveller were to visit Athens today, what would he see?

The Propylaea, the Parthenon and the Erechtheum are still standing, though badly damaged. The tragedy is that the Parthenon stood almost intact until the seventeenth century. Athens was being attacked and the Parthenon was being used as a store for gunpowder. During the attack a shell struck the Parthenon and the gunpowder exploded. The temple was very badly damaged. Archaeologists have worked very hard to restore parts of the temple. It is no small tribute to the skill of the Greek craftsmen that so much was left standing despite the explosion. Some of the sculptures were rescued and can be seen today in a small museum near the Parthenon. Some were also recovered last century by the British Ambassador, Lord Elgin, and these can be seen today in the British Museum in London. They are now called The Elgin Marbles.

The Parthenon still stands proudly

Although damaged, the Parthenon still stands proudly,

watching over Athens—a sight so impressive that thousands of tourists flock to the city each year to view its magnificent grandeur. At night it is often floodlit to create a lasting impression of haunting beauty.

It is not difficult, after seeing the Parthenon, to understand why architects and builders all over the world, in different centuries, have tried to imitate the simple, yet elegant style of

The Acropolis floodlit *(above left)*

Sculpture of a horse's head—one of the Elgin marbles, now in the British Museum *(above)*

The Parthenon and Erechtheum today

A Greek Thomson church in Glasgow

Greek architecture. One Scottish architect, Alexander Thomson, produced so many designs and buildings based on the Greek style that he was called Greek Thomson.

Many kinds of buildings all over the world, from the Congress Buildings in Washington DC to private houses in Glasgow owe a great debt to the Ancient Greeks. Such is the legacy they have left us.

The Capitol building, Washington D.C.

Front doors with Greek style decorative columns

Things to do:

Write the heading *Greek Architecture*

Section A

1 How would you recognize a building based on the Greek style of architecture? Draw a sketch to illustrate your answer.

2 Make a list (with a short description of each) of all the buildings you have seen yourself which are built according to the Greek style. If you have any photographs (perhaps you could even take some yourself of suitable buildings in your neighbourhood), paste them into your notebook.

   You could also collect some postcards of buildings in other countries where the Greek style has been used. If you have an old travel brochure, look up the section on Greece and cut out any pictures of Greek buildings. Keep them in your notebook.

3 Draw the three designs used for the column. Colour your drawings and name each one.

   How did the Greeks construct a tall column?

5 Draw or trace a picture of the Parthenon. Colour your drawing. Underneath your drawing, write a short paragraph naming the building and explaining where you would find it, what use it had, to whom it was dedicated, what it was made from, and what style of column was used.

6 Write a sentence or two to explain (a) pediment; (b) frieze.

7 What was unusual about the building on the Acropolis called the Erechtheum? Make a drawing to illustrate your answer.

8 Where in the United Kingdom can you see some of the sculptures used to decorate the Parthenon? What are they called?

Section B

1 This is an activity for the whole class. Construct your own frieze for wall-display. Some of you will draw and paint the background—the streets and houses of Athens leading up to the Acropolis. Others, in small groups, will draw, paint and cut out (ready for pasting on the background) horses, riders, chariots, animals, girls, crowds, priests and anyone else who took part in the great procession.

2 It is not too difficult to make a small model of the Parthenon, using only scrap materials. On the next page is a rough plan for you to follow.

TEMPLE

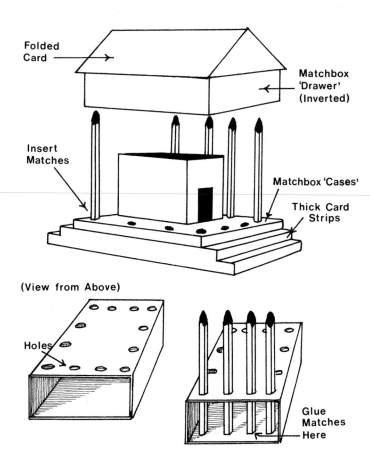

Folded Card

Matchbox 'Drawer' (Inverted)

Insert Matches

Matchbox 'Cases'

Thick Card Strips

(View from Above)

Holes

Glue Matches Here

10 Life in Athens

Houses and furniture

Demosthenes, the Athenian orator, has this to say about Greek houses:

> The great men of old built splendid edifices for the use of the State, and set up beautiful works of art which later ages can never match. In private life, however, they were severe and simple and the dwelling of a nobleman like Aristides or Miltiades was no more sumptuous than that of an ordinary citizen.

The illustration on the next page of the house at Dystus, on the island of Euboea, shows clearly the distinguishing features common to all Greek houses and the simplicity to which Demosthenes refers.

With what materials is the house built?

Simply with those readily available or easy to produce, thereby making the house relatively inexpensive to build. There is at the base of the walls a solid foundation of stone. Above this, the walls consist of brick made from sun-baked clay. The frames of the doors and windows are made of wood and the roofs are covered with sun-baked clay tiles. Constructed to a simple plan, the house offers both privacy and protection. It looks inwards on itself and is built so as to exclude the noise and inquisitiveness of the people outside, to block out the heat and glare of the sun, and to keep out the dust in the narrow streets.

This house is quite unlike our modern house. There is no front door, but instead a long porch or covered passageway leading in from the street outside. This passageway narrows towards the main door; a second door is placed a few yards inside. The passageway then passes the porter's room into an open courtyard which contains a well. It is quite easy to see that it was virtually impossible to enter unannounced so that

The house at Dystus

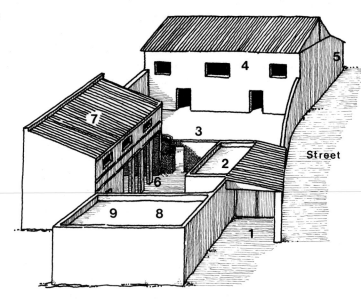

1. Entrance
2. Porter's Room
3. Courtyard
4. ANDRON
5. Bedrooms
6. EXEDRA
7. Women's Bedrooms
8. Kitchen
9. Loom-room

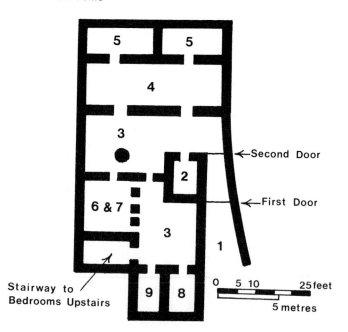

Second Door

First Door

Stairway to
Bedrooms Upstairs

0 5 10   25 feet

5 metres

the women would have been quite safe while their husbands were out for most of the day on business.

To the right of the courtyard lies the Andron or men's dining-room, behind this two smaller bedrooms. The rooms to the left of the courtyard are separated from the main courtyard by two doors and this area of the house was allocated to the women, the maid servants, and children whenever male guests were present in the Andron being entertained. In the section of the house portioned off for the ladies, there is a recess or Exedra where they could sit in the summer and upstairs various bedrooms reached by stairs in the Exedra.

This arrangement of the house into rooms solely for men and rooms solely for women is quite a common feature in Greek houses and numerous references in their literature confirm this:

> My little house is divided into a ground and upper floor, partitioned in the same places; the lower rooms are for men's use and the upper for women's use. After our child was born, however, his mother nursed him, and to save her the dangerous descent of the stairs whenever he had to be washed, I installed myself on the upper floor and the women on the ground.
>
> (*Lysias* I, 9)

Women working at loom

Women, except for a few occasions, spent most of their time in the house and much of their time was taken up making cloth in the loom-room.

The women bought the wool directly from the shepherd and they themselves completed the whole process of converting the wool into cloth. The married women attended to the more difficult task of weaving while their daughters did the spinning. Weather permitting, this work could also be done in the open courtyard or in the shade of the Exedra if the sun was too strong, and we can imagine them working away while their favourite dog or hen might wander through the room, and picture their small children sitting in the corner watching closely the work of their mother.

In addition to this manufacturing of cloth, other articles were often produced in larger houses with more rooms available. One or two of these rooms were set aside as work-rooms where skilled slaves made furniture or shoes or pottery. Very often, however, the owner of the house found that it was more profitable to convert these work-rooms into shops cut off from the rest of the house with their own doors on the street and rent them to freeborn craftsmen.

Whenever male guests visited the house, they were received

in the Andron or the dining-room, and on these occasions the women confined themselves to the seclusion of their own rooms. Placed around the walls of the Andron were couches on which the men reclined as they enjoyed their meal and this was followed by their famous after-dinner drinking parties—(symposia).

Dining scene

Since these parties extended late into the evening, lighting was required. The lamps they used were small round containers with an opening in the middle for pouring in the oil, a spout at one end for the wick, and a handle at the other end.

The floors of the Andron were often covered in very simple, yet beautiful mosaics. These were made in uncut pebbles of two or three colours and most of them represent mythological scenes framed in borders of elaborate patterns.

For decoration, wreaths of flowers were hung on the walls as well as long streamers of vine and ivy. To brighten the drabness of the plain clay brick, they applied to the walls a preparation of stucco or fine plaster on which patterns were painted or scenes from mythology. Tapestries too, which the women produced in their own house, were draped from the ceilings to create softness and warmth.

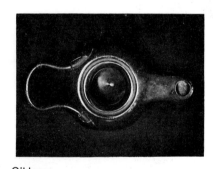

Oil lamp

In one of Aristophanes's plays, he gives prudent advice about what a guest should say to please his host:

Stretch out your knees and shed yourself in an easy way along the cushions, then praise some piece of furniture, gaze at the patterns on the ceiling and admire the tapestries.

This decoration, however modest when compared to a modern house, was confined to the Andron; the other rooms observed the customary simplicity and severity and the golden rule of nothing to excess.

If the owner was rich enough to have a room set aside as a bathroom, there was a drain from it linking up with a drain from the Andron, and one from the latrine (usually situated in the courtyard) discharging into a common drain in the street outside. The Greeks were very concerned about cleanliness. Our word 'hygiene' is derived from the Greek word ὑγιεια which means cleanliness. Not all houses, however, possessed their own well inside the house and water had to be fetched from common fountains generously provided throughout the city. These were very popular places for the exchange of gossip among women, the most famous fountain in Athens being the Enneakrounos (nine-mouthed) with nine lions heads through which water spouted.

Women fetching water

Greek furniture

There was very little furniture in a Greek house. It consisted simply of chairs, stools, couches, tables and chests. Since there was no mass-production of furniture, every article had to be hand-made. Occasionally their furniture was made of bronze, but mostly of wood and in the countryside there was a generous supply of this material. Maple, beech, willow, citron, cedar, oak and many other types of wood were plentiful. When he was making a piece of furniture, the Greek carpenter restricted himself to a few simple designs, but added his own touch of decoration to make the product a work of art.

The Greek chair (klismos) with its curving back and legs was very light, comfortable and elegant.

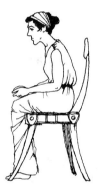
A klismos

The seat consisted of interlacing thongs on which a cushion could be placed. Ladies particularly, when using a klismos, liked to have a footstool. These footstools, with their own intricate carving, could also be used for stepping on to a high couch.

In addition to the klismos, they had also various types of stools. One type was a stool without a back and with four legs. The stool was easy to carry and consequently very popular. They had also another type of stool with legs which instead of being perpendicular crossed as in a modern folding stool.

The Greek couch (κλινη) was used both for sleeping and reclining during meals. The Greek couch regularly had a headboard and often a low foot-board resembling the modern bed. The mattress was placed on a frame of interlacing cords similar to that seen in the klismos. Covers and pillows were also used. It seems from the many paintings of couches in Greek vases that

Men on stools

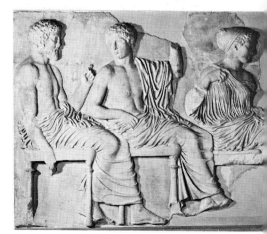

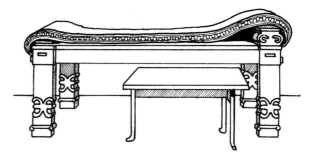

a bed was not 'made up' as nowadays with sheets and covers tucked in. Instead, the covers were merely laid on top of the couch.

The Greeks had fewer uses for tables than we have. The table was used simply during meals to support dishes and food. It was put alongside the couch of the person reclining and when the meal was finished, it was carried away or pushed under the couch. Each person had his own individual table. The top was usually oblong resting on three legs. It was light, plain and low.

There were no wardrobes or closets in a Greek house. Instead,

Folding stool *(above)*

Couch and table *(above right)*

Woman placing garments in chest

they put away their clothing, jewellery and other personal belongings in chests. Clothes were kept in large chests; jewellery and cosmetics were kept in small and dainty ones. There were also no cupboards and many of the things, which we would put in a cupboard, had to be hung on the walls. Life in a Greek house was simple and uncomplicated.

Things to do:

Section A

1   Fill in the blanks in the following paragraph:
    Greek houses were various in size and shape. However, they all had common features. A person entered a Greek house along a short .... from the street and from there into a .... where there was a well. One of the most important rooms in the house was called a .... where the women made cloth. The other important room was called the .... where they ate and had their famous dining parties called .... Here the men reclined on .... where they feasted and were entertained. Greek floors had no carpets but they were decorated with .... They sat on stools and they had a chair called .... Their clothes were stored in ....

2   Make drawings of (a) a stool; (b) a chair; (c) a chest.

3   Copy the plan of a Greek house.

Section B

1   Make a design for a Greek mosaic. With this design as a guide make up the mosaic, using coloured paper or painted egg shells.

2   Make a list of the things a modern housewife uses which Greek women did not know about.

3   The Greeks had many slaves. How would they be used in the house?

4   Imagine yourself as a woman in Ancient Greece. What sort of things do you think you would have to do around the house?

Food and meals

The Ancient Athenians had a very plain and simple diet. Their staple foods were bread, fish, eggs, poultry and vegetables.

Bread was made at home. The grain was ground down by the women who rubbed a stone backwards and forwards in a shallow tray, reducing the grain to a coarse flour. This was made into dough which was kneaded on a special table and then baked, either beneath a domed tile with hot ashes heaped on top, or in a small oven heated from below.

Fish was very plentiful. No part of Attica was very far from the sea and in the Mediterranean there are many different varieties of fish.

Fisherman in Rhodes mending nets

Fishermen today on small Greek island

Plate showing different types of seafood

When a catch arrived in the harbour, a bell was rung so that everyone could come to buy fresh fish. The fish could be eaten the same day, or else salted and kept in jars for later use. The picture shows a plate with drawings of several types of fish caught by the Greek sailors.

The Athenians, like all other Greeks, ate beef only on very special occasions, such as at a religious ceremony when a bull was sacrificed to a god. The mountainous nature of their country prevented the Greeks from keeping large herds of beef-cattle. The rough, upland country, however, was ideal

84

for rearing goats and sheep which produced a small amount of meat and, perhaps more important, milk for making into cheese. The goat-skins were useful for making into leather, and the sheep were sheared to produce wool for cloth. Most families tried to keep a few pigs since pork was popular. Bacon and lard could also be obtained from pigs.

Butcher's shop

Poultry could be reared easily, even in small households inside the city, and this provided an additional source of meat for an Athenian family.

Vegetables such as peas, beans, cabbage, lettuce, lentils, leeks, and onions were common, along with a wide variety of fruit and nuts. Especially plentiful in Attica was the olive whose oil was used for cooking and as a substitute for butter. It also had many other uses, including lighting. It was even rubbed into the skin during bathing instead of soap! Grapes were also plentiful and were used to produce wine. This was widely drunk, as it still is in most Mediterranean countries, and was particularly popular in ancient times as there was no tea or coffee. The Greeks did not like strong drink and so they mixed the wine, which was thick and syrupy, with water before serving. The usual mixture was two parts water to one of wine. The Greeks thought it rude and lacking in manners to drink too much. One writer commented:

85

The first glass of wine stands for health; the second stands for pleasure; the third means sleep and then sensible men go away home; the fourth means rudeness, the fifth shouting, the sixth disorder in the streets; the seventh produces black eyes; the eight brings a police summons.

Aristophanes, in one of his comic plays, says:

Drinking is bad; For wine means banging at doors, hitting people and have to pay for it—and a headache into the bargain.

A man returns drunk from a party; his wife waits anxiously behind the door

Sugar was unknown to the Greeks. They used honey instead for sweetening. The honey produced in Attica was especially famous.

The Greeks had several methods of cooking their food.

They could grill, or roast with the meat fixed to a spit. They could fry in hot olive oil. Sometimes they boiled their food or casseroled it in containers of liquid.

Like the food, Athenian meals were generally very simple. Breakfast was eaten extremely early as most Greeks got up at dawn and it consisted only of a piece of bread dipped in wine! This had to last them until mid-day when they had lunch. This was a light meal of bread, figs, olives and occasionally fish. The main meal of the day was dinner, eaten in the late afternoon or early evening. The first course was usually made up of fish or poultry. This was accompanied by vegetables cooked in oil or served with sauces. The diners had no knives or forks: they used their fingers instead! Spoons were sometimes used when shellfish were on the menu. All the shells, bones and scraps were thrown on to the floor. The second course consisted of nuts, olives, figs, grapes and other fruits.

One of the highlights of Athenian social life was the dinner-party. A rich Athenian loved to invite several of his friends to dinner. Only men were invited and the women of the house would not attend the dinner-party. The dining-room, lit by oil lamps, was arranged with couches: the Greeks reclined on these when eating, propping themselves up on cushions.

Slaves met the guests when they first arrived. These slaves took the guests' sandals and poured scented water over their feet to remove any dust gathered while walking through the streets. The guests were then led into the dining-room where they took up position on the couches, and waited for the first course to be served. Slaves brought the food in on small tables, one for each guest. These were placed alongside the couches. The guests ate heartily since this was their main meal of the day. When they had finished the first course, the slaves re-appeared and removed the small tables. Others swept the floor, clearing away all the scraps and bones. One slave went round with water so that the guests could wash their hands. When all this was done, the tables were brought back in, laden with nuts and fruits for dessert.

With these two courses now over, the second part of the dinner could now begin. This was the 'symposium' or 'drinking-together'. The host poured out some wine in honour of the gods and a slave brought in wreaths of flowers for each guest to wear round his head. A hymn was sung and then wine was served to all the guests. Often someone was chosen by lot, or by the throw of the dice, to take charge of the 'symposium'. It was this man, called the 'symposiarch', who decided how much water should be mixed with the wine.

During the 'symposium', the guests loved to talk and to

Flute girl at a banquet

discuss all manner of subjects. Often flute-girls, dancers and acrobats were provided for entertainment.

Xenophon describes such entertainment:

The girl began to accompany the dancer on the flute, and a boy at her elbow handed her up the hoops until he had given her twelve. She took these and as she danced kept throwing them whirling into the air and catching them again in regular rhythm. . . . Then there was brought in a hoop set all around with upright swords; over these the dancer turned somersaults, into the hoop and out again, as the diners looked on in amazement, afraid that she might hurt herself. But she completed her performance fearlessly and safely.

Just as often, the diners made their own entertainment, organized by the 'symposiarch'. A favourite form of past-time was asking riddles, each guest asking one in turn. Another popular entertainment was singing accompanied by music from the lyre. The songs were called 'skolia' or 'drinking-songs' and were sung by each man in turn, one taking over where the other left off. Here are a few excerpts from some 'skolia':

'Wreath with me, drink with me, play with me, love with
me as well.
Be wild when I am wild, and sober when I've a sober spell.'

'There's a scorpion under every stone: he'll sting you
lurking there.
For there's no treachery but waits upon the unseen: beware.'

'The sow, she wanted the acorn, and on it at last she'll dine.
But I, I wanted this fair maid, and now at last she's mine.'

Even more light-hearted entertainment could be arranged, especially if the 'symposiarch' had a mischievous sense of fun: a bald-headed man might be asked to comb his hair; a man with a stammer might be ordered to make a speech; or a bold young man might be ordered to seize the flute-girl and race round the room with her in his arms!

The 'symposium' often continued well into the night, with music, riddles, singing, and perhaps most important of all, when all the other entertainments had paled, good conversation.

I propose that we send away the flute-girl and entertain ourselves with conversation. If you ask on what subject, I've a proposal to make on that too. . . . My friend Phaedros is always saying that it's a shame that other gods have hymns and songs of praise addressed to them by the poets, while no one has ever composed a song in honour of so mighty a god as Love. I think that Phaedros is right . . . and I feel that we should honour this god. If you agree, we shall not need anything beyond conversation to occupy us; my proposal is that each of us, going from left to right, should make the best speech he can in praise of love, and that Phaedros should begin since it was originally his idea.

(From Plato's *Symposium*)

And so they begin, speaking, listening, questioning, debating, far into the night.

Things to do:

Section A

1 Write down the heading *Food*. Underline. Now answer these questions in sentences.
   (a) What were the staple foods in the diet of the Ancient Athenians? What are our staple foods today?
   (b) What does the word 'protein' mean? (If you are not sure, look up the word in a dictionary or ask your teacher to help.) What was the main source of protein in the Athenians' diet?
   (c) Why was beef not common in Greece? When was it eaten?
   (d) What foodstuffs did the Greeks obtain from (i) goats; (ii) sheep; (iii) pigs?
   (e) What vegetables did the Athenians like?
   (f) What uses did olive-oil have?
   (g) What was used instead of (i) tea and coffee; (ii) sugar?
   (h) Why did the Greeks have no tea, coffee or sugar?

2 This time your heading is *Cooking*. Underline. Now write a short paragraph comparing and contrasting Greek methods of cooking with those we use today.

3 Your heading is *Meals*. Underline. Now write out the following paragraph, filling in the blanks:
   Athenian meals were very simple. Breakfast was just .... Lunch was eaten at .... and consisted of .... The main meal, or ......, was eaten during .... There were .... courses: the first was ....; the second was ....

Section B

1 Imagine that you have been invited to attend a dinner-party to be held in Ancient Athens. Write an essay des-

89

cribing what you have to eat, what you see and hear, what entertainment you enjoy.

2 Draw a scene to illustrate some part of a dinner-party.

3 Design a menu-card and on it compose a menu for a dinner-party, using only foods known to the Ancient Athenians.

4 Find out about the food of other people, ancient and modern. Perhaps you could collect menus from various restaurants near you (e.g. Indian, Chinese, French, Italian, etc.) and arrange them for display on a wall-chart. Similarly, you could find out about wines—what are the different types; where do they come from, etc.? You could collect labels from wine-bottles for display on a wall-chart.

Doric chiton

The sort of clothes men wore

Dress and fashion

In Greece today the weather is very hot for most of the year and the people do not need as many clothes as we do in our colder, northern climate. The same was true of the Ancient Greeks. Their clothes were very simple both in material and design. The cloth, usually wool or linen, was woven at home by the women. Many colours were used and amongst the most popular were purple, violet, saffron and red, Sometimes the cloth was decorated with stars or spots. Occasionally, a meandering scroll-like design was used round the edges.

The main garment worn by women was the 'chiton', a type of loose-fitting dress. There were two main styles—Doric or Ionic. The Doric was made very simply. It consisted of a large piece of cloth, usually wool, which was folded. It was then placed round the body. It was fastened on the shoulders by brooches and then allowed to fall into folds. A belt, often called a girdle, was worn round the waist to hold the dress in position. An extra-long dress of this style was called 'peplos'. The Ionic style was more like a modern dress. The material, most often linen, was folded and sewn, leaving holes for the head and arms. Again a belt was worn to keep the dress in position and to encourage it to fall into attractive folds from the waist down.

Over the 'chiton' could be worn the 'himation'—a kind of shawl or cloak. This was especially useful outside on a cool evening in autumn when the sun had gone down.

Men's clothing was, if anything, even simpler. Their most important garment was a short version of the 'chiton', also belted at the waist.

The right shoulder was often left bare if the man was taking

exercise or doing some hard work. The 'himation' was also used, especially outside or on long journeys. This cloak was fastened at the shoulder, often with a beautiful brooch.

On solemn, formal occasions, a long robe was worn with the right shoulder often left bare.

Young children hardly ever wore clothes. As they grew older, girls began to wear a simple sort of smock to above the knee. Boys, when ready to go to school wore garments similar to the man's 'chiton' described above.

At home people went barefoot, but in the streets or when travelling, they wore leather sandals. These were very simple and usually made to measure—the man or woman went to the

Patterned costumes *(above left)*

Ionian chiton *(above)*, with himation *(below)*, showing way of fitting

91

A slave carrying a sunshade

Various Greek hairstyles

A gold necklace

cobbler's shop and placed his foot on a piece of leather, and the sole was cut out round the foot. The sole was attached to the foot by leather thongs tied across the instep and round the ankle.

Headwear was not common, although a man going on a long journey often wore the 'petasos', a wide-brimmed, felt hat. A woman was often protected from the hot sun by a parasol which a slave held over her head. Also, the 'himation' could be brought up to cover the head if necessary.

Hair was worn in a variety of elaborate styles. It was often arranged in great masses of ringlets and gathered on top of the head. Ribbons, veils or small caps were used to hold the hair in position. Sometimes the ringlets were allowed to hang down in long strands. Combs were used for hairdressing. They were made of wood or ivory and were often delicately carved. It was not unknown for some women to dye their hair in order to obtain a colour they liked better.

Jewellery was very popular with women. They wore rings, necklaces, earrings and bracelets (not only at the wrist, but between elbow and shoulder as well). Some women wore a type of bracelet round their ankles.

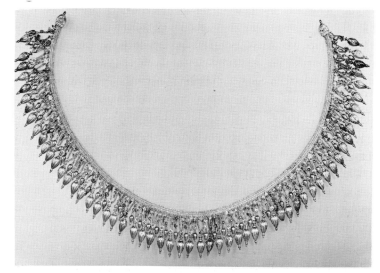

Gold earrings, *(left)* 4th century BC, *(right)* 6th century BC

A gold earring, 4th century BC *(above left)*
Gold earrings, 3rd century BC *(above)*

Woman with compact

Make-up was used just as much as it is nowadays. White lead was used to whiten the skin—a white skin was regarded as a sign of beauty—and alkanet juice was used to highlight the cheeks with a slight hint of rose-colour, just as rouge is used today. Lipstick was also known, and eye shadow (probably made from ashes of some type!) was popular. Some women tended to overdo the effect and one poet tells of the hazards:

If you go out in the hot summer weather, two streaks of black run from your eyes; sweat, running from your cheeks, carves a red furrow all the way down your neck; and when your hair touches your neck, it covers it with white-lead.

Some husbands disapproved of their wives using make-up. We read of one husband who, after finding his wife wearing make-up, was angry and gave her a lecture:

Please realize that I do not prefer white paint and alkanet juice to your real colour. Humans find the human body most delightful when it is undisguised.

He then goes on to say that she will look better if she works hard in the house.

Work and exercise will give you a better appetite, improve your health and add *natural* colour to your cheeks.

Things to do:

Section A

1 Write down as your heading *Women's Dress*. Underline.
Draw or trace pictures of women wearing (a) the Doric style; (b) the Ionic style.
Colour both drawings, using the correct colour-schemes.
Label each drawing and then write a short paragraph to describe each method of dress—type of material, colour, size, how sewn or fastened etc.

2 Write down as your heading *Men's Dress*. Underline.
Draw or trace pictures to illustrate the various types of men's clothing. Colour your drawings and write a short paragraph to explain what you have drawn.

3 The heading is *Shoes*. Underline. Answer these questions:
   (a) How were shoes made?
   (b) How were they made to fit the foot?
   (c) What material was used?
   (d) Where were shoes worn/not worn?

4 Put as the heading *Make-up*. Underline.
On one page of your note-book list all the items used by girls today for make-up and mention the purpose each item serves. Illustrate with advertisements or photographs cut from magazines. On the opposite page of your note-book list all the items used by an Athenian woman for make-up and the purpose they served. If you can, draw a picture to illustrate this page. Include hair-styles as part of this item.

Section B

1 An activity for a small group. Make a wall-chart called 'Fashion Then & Now'. With drawings, paintings, photographs, even original designs, illustrate the changing fashions of Ancient Athens and today.

2 Make a cardboard figure which will stand. Try to dress the figure in the Greek style using a handkerchief, cloth or paper.

3 Make a mobile to hang from the ceiling with four or five figures, each with a different type of dress. Include both male and female dress.

4 Compose an imaginary conversation between a modern woman (a follower of Women's Lib.?) and the Greek husband who disapproved of make-up.

A wedding

Girls in Ancient Greece were married shortly after their fifteenth birthday, to men considerably older than themselves. Sometimes, a man did not actually see his bride until the day of the wedding. His father chose her, often for social, financial or even business reasons. There were also professional match-makers, usually widows, who knew which girls came from wealthy families.

The engagement or betrothal was a solemn contract between the future husband and the girl's father, who not only promised his daughter's hand in marriage but also agreed to give a dowry, a present (usually of money), to the newly-wed couple. The girl herself was sometimes not even present at the betrothal ceremony!

The wedding followed soon after the engagement. On the day before the ceremony the young girl, often no more than a child, dedicated all her toys and playthings to Artemis. She then bathed in water drawn from a special holy spring. This was supposed to purify her. She was helped in her preparations by her bridesmaid, often an older woman who could give advice. On the day of the wedding, the bride wore a special dress and a veil over her head. Sacrifice and prayer took place at the family altar. This was followed by a banquet where a wedding-cake, made from crushed sesame seed and honey, was eaten.

Preparations for the wedding

In the evening came the 'fetching-home' procession when the bridegroom, attended by his best man, took the bride to his house. Flute players led the way as the newly-wed couple

95

Marriage ceremony

A wedding procession

were driven to their home in a chariot. The bride's parents and friends walked behind the chariot singing and carrying pine-torches. As the couple entered their new home, which was decorated with olive and laurel boughs, nuts and dried figs were thrown over them, just as today we throw confetti. The bride was offered a piece of quince, or a date—both symbols of fertility. All the friends then went away leaving the new husband and his wife alone together.

Next day another feast was held. Friends came to congratulate the newly-weds and to offer them presents. It was then also that the bride's father paid his daughter's dowry.

Like us, the Ancient Greeks had many jokes about getting married, and often one man will advise another not to get married: nothing could be worse!

— If you've got any sense, you won't leave the life you lead, and marry. Why, I've been married myself and know what I'm advising against.
— It's all settled. Let the die be cast.
— Right, go ahead, but I hope you come out safe. You're hurling yourself into a sea of tossing troubles, not the Libyan or the Aegean, where three boats out of thirty escape calamity. Not one man, who's married, has ever been saved, not one of them at all.

(From the Greek comic playwright, Menander)

Things to do:

Section A

1 Write down as your heading *A Wedding in Athens*. Answer these questions carefully in sentences. Try to join all the answers together to form a piece of continuous information.

(a) How old was a girl when she was married in Ancient Greece?
(b) How old was her husband?
(c) Who often arranged the wedding? Why did this person want to arrange it?
(d) What preparations did the bride make before her wedding?
(e) What happened on the day of the wedding?
(f) What was the 'fetching-home'?
(g) What did the Greeks throw instead of confetti? When was this thrown?
(h) What happened on the day after the wedding?

Section B
1 Draw and colour a picture of the 'fetching-home' procession.
2 Why do you think that a piece of quince, or a date, was offered to the bride?
3 Collect some photographs of a modern wedding and paste them into your notebook. Perhaps you could design a wedding invitation for yourself.

Women's life

The Law of Ancient Athens considered a woman to be the property first of her father and later of her husband. A woman was not expected to take any part in public life. She was barred from the Ecclesia. The affairs of the State were solely the concern of the men.

Being denied such opportunities to take an active part in public life, an Athenian woman could devote all her energies and attention to the running of the house where she was in absolute control. She was expected to be able to cook, spin, weave, bring up the children and manage the family budget. She had been trained for these tasks since she was a young girl.

If she belonged to a wealthy family, she would have a retinue of slaves to do most of the routine jobs in the house. An important part of her activities was to be able to control these slaves and to organize work for them to do. Xenophon describes some of a woman's main duties in the house:

Your duties will be to remain indoors and to send out those servants whose work is outside and to superintend those who are to work inside. You are to receive the income of the house and to distribute as much of it as has to be spent, and you must keep some in reserve. Take care that the sum laid by for a year is not spent in a month. When wool is brought

Mother and daughter cooking 97

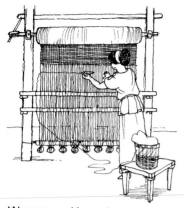

Woman working at loom

A Greek Lady

to you, you must see that clothes are made for them who want them. You must also see to it that the corn is dry and in good condition for making food.

A poor woman was not so lucky. She would have to work long, hard hours to make ends meet, with little or no help from slaves. Aristophanes tells of a woman who had lost her husband:

My husband died in Cyprus and left me with five young children to look after. It was as much as I could do to keep them alive. I had to sell sprigs of myrtle at a stall in the market.

In addition to her weak legal position, an Athenian woman was socially handicapped in certain ways. She often had to retire to her own special quarters in the house; she could not attend any dinner-party given by her husband for his friends. Some men probably believed that their wives should say as little as possible and keep out of sight. Pericles, in his most famous speech, declared that 'the best reputation a woman can have is not to be spoken of among men, either for good or evil'.

Many other men, however, must have treated their wives with respect and love. For them, women had an important role to play in the life of the home. Many vase-paintings have been found with scenes of domestic life. Some of these are urns used at funerals to contain the ashes of a loved one, and they often show a painting of a wife (now dead) bidding a last, fond farewell to her husband, children and slaves. Tombstones also have been found carved with similar scenes.

Xenophon tells of one man called Ischomachus who wants to treat his wife as a loved and trusted partner, in no way inferior to himself:

... feel confident that with the advancing years the better partner you prove to me, and the better mother to our children, the greater will be the honour paid to you in our home.

It seems quite reasonable to suppose that a society which could produce such great plays as 'Antigone' and 'Medea' (in which female characters play important and decisive roles) must have treated its womenfolk with no small measure of respect.

Things to do:

Section A

1 The heading at the top of your page should be *Women's Life*. Below is a summary of this topic in skeleton form. Try to expand it into a continuous piece of information, with two or three paragraphs.

The Law of Ancient Athens — property of father or husband — no part in public life — time for the house — duties in house — slaves to help (or not?) — social handicap — Pericles' opinion — respect and love — evidence of vase-paintings — female characters in plays.

Section B

1 Draw and colour a picture of a woman at work. Describe what you have drawn.

2 Who, in your opinion, would have made the better husband—Pericles or Ischomachus? Give reasons for your opinion.

3 An opportunity for a class debate, boys against girls! The motion is: 'Modern women have too much freedom and a return to the situation preferred by Pericles is desired.'

Birth and childhood

When a baby was born in Ancient Athens, the father inspected it closely. If he found that the child was weak or deformed in any way, he could order it to be left outside to die. If the child was strong and healthy, it would be received warmly into the family.

When a boy was born an olive branch was set over the door of the house. A woollen ribbon was used if it was a girl. Ten days after the birth the whole family gathered for a feast. A sacrifice was made and the child was named.

The child's early years were spent in the home, under the careful supervision of the mother. A wealthy family would have a nurse to help.

A wicker-work basket was used as a cradle. Some families had high-chairs for their children. Some of these chairs were not unlike those we have today, and an actual example found in the market-place in Athens was designed to hold a chamber-pot underneath.

Mother and nurse told their children all sorts of folk tales and conjured up stories of bogy-men who would come and take the children away if they misbehaved. Stories about

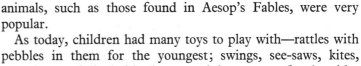

animals, such as those found in Aesop's Fables, were very popular.

As today, children had many toys to play with—rattles with pebbles in them for the youngest; swings, see-saws, kites, tops, hoops, dolls, hobby-horses, miniature carts for the older children. Boys were encouraged to build models: in Aristophanes' 'Clouds', a proud father mentions how clever his son is at making 'houses and ships and wagons and frogs out of bits of leather'.

Many different kinds of games were played, including leap-frog, piggy-back, and a form of Blind Man's Buff. Both boys and girls played with dice and knucklebones. These knucklebones were five small bones, attractively decorated and carved. They were thrown into the air, one at a time, and had to be caught and held on the back of the hand. Ball-games were popular too.

Children's toys (above)

Children playing with knuckle-bones (above right)

Doll with moveable arms and legs (right)

A mother with her child (far right)

100

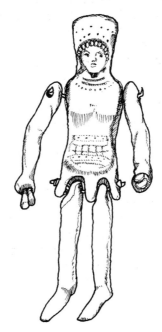

Pets were as common with children in Greece as they are today. A child might have a pet dog, a tortoise or even a hare. Sometimes a bird like a cock or quail was kept. This could be used in a cruel way to fight against another bird.

During the early years of childhood the mother was in charge. Her job was to provide a happy, secure home in which the children could live and play safely together.

Boy with a pet quail

Things to do:

Section A

1 Write as the heading for this section *Birth and Childhood*. Answer these questions in sentences or short paragraphs:
   (a) Nowadays it is illegal to kill a child once it is born. How did the practice of the Ancient Athenians differ?
   (b) Who supervised the children in their earliest years?
   (c) Write a paragraph to describe the toys, games and activities enjoyed by children in Athens. Draw some pictures to illustrate your paragraph.

Section B

1 What toys, games and activities are popular with children today? What are the main differences, and similarities, between today and the time of Ancient Athens?

Cock fighting

Schools and education

At about six years of age the life of a boy took a different course from that of his sister. Girls stayed at home under the supervision of their mothers and began to receive instruction in the skills of running a household—cooking, spinning, weaving and the supervision of slaves. Girls never went to school to receive a formal education or to be taught how to read and write. In contrast to this, boys started attending a proper school at the age of six or seven. This was the equivalent of our primary school. It was not compulsory to send a boy to school, but most fathers tried to do so for as long as they could afford it.

Lessons in this first school were held in the open air, or possibly in a building hired for the purpose. Elementary teachers were allowed to charge fees like any other businessman. As even poor boys received some form of elementary education, the fees were probably quite low, but when all the fees were added together they must have provided the teachers with a moderate income. A successful teacher might employ a slave or two to assist him.

The furniture and equipment in such schools was very sparse. There were chairs for the masters and stools for the pupils. There were no desks or tables. The pupils had no jotters or notebooks. Instead they used wax-tablets which they rested on their knees. They scratched the wax on the tablet with a stilus, a pointed stick tipped with iron or bone, and in this way they were able to write their exercises. The top of the stilus was flattened for smoothing out mistakes on the wax surface. In place of books, scrolls of papyrus were used. Papyrus, which gives us our word 'paper', was an early type of paper made from papyrus reeds. The reeds were opened up and the inside taken out. The reeds were then laid in rows and hammered. This made them stick together. More reeds were next placed on top and hammered in the same way. The result of this process was a coarse paper which could be used for making books. Such books were just continuous rolls of paper, often as much as thirty feet long. Writing was done in narrow columns. The ends were often decorated with ornately carved pieces of wood.

Writing tablet, scroll-book, stilus and book case

The school day probably began early. There is an old Athenian law which tried to stop teachers opening their schools before sunrise. The boys were accompanied to school by an old, trusted slave who was called 'paidagogos' or 'boy-keeper'. Each wealthy family had one 'paidagogos' to look after all the sons in the family. It was his responsibility to see that the boys got to school safely, behaved well in the streets and did not play truant (though one of the pictures shows that he may occasionally have failed in his duty!) He carried a long cane, presumably to beat the boys if they misbehaved. Misbehaviour inside the school was not tolerated and teachers often used corporal punishment. Such punishment was inflicted with a cane or, perhaps more commonly, with a sandal. The 'paidagogos' also carried the boys' writing-tablets and musical instruments. He sat in the classroom during the lesson, listening to every word, so that he could help, if necessary, with the boys' homework.

Teacher belting a boy with a sandal!

Paidagogos

A truant prefers fishing to school!

103

The main items in a boy's education were reading, writing, music and physical education. Reading and writing were taught by the 'grammatistes'. The first task was to learn by heart the names of the letters of the alphabet. Sometimes, to make this task easier, the alphabet was set to music. One teacher, to make reading and spelling easier, invented a 'spelling-drama' where the spelling was acted out as if in a play, with each boy representing a letter. Reading itself was a more difficult task than it is today for there were no spaces between the words and no punctuation. Writing perhaps was easier for most of the boys, but some had difficulty in writing in straight lines. Plato tells us how

> writing-masters draw lines with their pens for those pupils who are still awkward at writing, and make them follow the direction of the lines when trying to write.

When the pupils had mastered their letters and were able to read, they began to study the works of the Greek poets. Plato describes how:

> the teacher sets before them the works of good poets for them to read, and makes them learn them by heart. He chooses poems which tell of the heroes of old and praise their deeds so that the boys may admire them and strive to copy them.

Homer was the most important poet studied in schools, and every schoolboy knew his two famous poems—'The Iliad' (about the Trojan War) and 'The Odyssey' (which tells of the wanderings and adventures of Odysseus after the fall of Troy). It was not uncommon to learn the whole of these two poems by heart—about 26 000 lines in all! One Athenian, called Niceratos, was proud of just such an achievement:

> My father, wishing to make me a good man, ordered me to learn by heart every line of Homer, and I believe that I can recite to you at this very moment the whole of 'The Iliad' and 'The Odyssey'.

The Greek schoolmaster believed that the writings of Homer and other poets were not just poems to be studied as literature— they were a means of teaching boys how to become good men and worthy citizens.

As well as teaching reading and writing, the 'grammatistes' almost certainly taught some arithmetic. The boys were probably taught enough simple arithmetic to be able to buy and sell in the market and to carry on a trade. The letters of the alphabet were used to represent figures. Simple reckoning

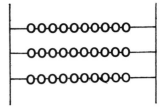

An abacus

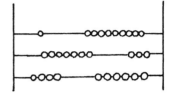

An abacus showing the number 936

Music and writing lessons; on the right sits the paidagogos (*above left*)

could be done on the fingers, but for more complicated calculations an abacus was used.

Music was considered an essential part of a boy's education, although a poor man might have decided to have his son taught only reading and writing, omitting the extra cost of music lessons. 'Kitharistes' was the name given to the music teacher. He taught the boys how to sing and how to play the lyre or the double-flute. Music played a more important part in the lives of the Athenians than it does today. Every Greek man, at some time or other, would be expected to entertain his friends at a dinner-party by singing or playing some instrument. Not to be able to do so was a sign that the man was lacking in education. As well as this, all Greek poetry was meant to be sung to the accompaniment of music. If the pupils were to be able to understand and appreciate the poetry of Homer properly, they would need some knowledge of music.

Music and reading lessons. Who is on the right?

Physical education played a prominent role in the education of the Athenian boy. The Greeks loved to take part in sport as it developed their bodies, and kept them beautiful and healthy. Sport also kept the men fit in case of war when they would have to join the army at a moment's notice. Every boy practised some form of physical education as soon as he started school, and he would continue to take an active part in sport after leaving school. The physical education teacher, or 'paidotribes', was an expert and, like a modern physiotherapist, he was expected to be able to prescribe the best exercises for each boy at each level. Physical education took place in a special training area, the 'palaestra', equipped for gymnastics and athletics. The exercise area was covered with sand. The 'paidotribes' carried a forked stick as a reminder of his power to inflict punishment should any of the boys try to misbehave or to cheat. He had assistants who played the flute since all exercise was done to musical accompaniment. This was to teach the boys how to move gracefully and with good rhythm. One assistant carried a pick-axe and worked on the sand, making it soft for those doing exercises.

On arrival at the 'palaestra' the boys took off all their clothes. All exercise was taken naked so that the 'paidotribes' could see how the body was developing and decide which exercises were necessary for correct development. The boys rubbed their skin with olive-oil to make their bodies supple. They were then ready to receive instruction in javelin- and discus-throwing, jumping, running, boxing and wrestling. After exercise, the boys hurried to the changing-rooms. There they used a scraper (strigil) to remove the sweat and dust before finally having a shower or a swim to clean themselves properly.

The Athenian schoolboy had holidays from school on certain days of the month when there were festivals in honour of the gods, or a procession with public games and contests. The month of Anthesterion (from mid-February to mid-March) was so crowded with holidays that one stingy parent saved himself the expense of fees by not sending his son to school at all during the whole of that month. Apart from these holidays, there were no continuous vacations, as we have today, unless a number of feast days came together.

Some boys succeeded in making extra holidays for themselves by playing truant. Herodes gives us a picture of a truant. His mother is worried and full of complaints:

Hoist up this wicked boy and thrash him till his blasted soul comes jumping through his mouth. He's wrecked the roof of his poor mother's head with pitch-and-toss. For knuckle-

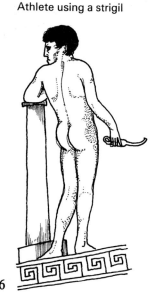

Athlete using a strigil

Wrestlers

bones won't satisfy him now, and everyday things go from bad to worse. He'd be hard put to find his writing-master's door but bills arrive each thirtieth of the month. Yet ask him where the gambling-den is, and in a breath he'll tell you. His poor writing-tablet that I spread and smooth so carefully each month with wax slips down between the bedpost and the wall. He scowls as though it were Death's self to see it, won't write a proper word but scrapes it clean. Yet in his satchel rattle lots of dice. . . .

Elementary or primary education probably finished when boys were about fourteen years old. Those boys whose parents were not rich then went to work to earn a living. Those with wealthy parents continued with a form of secondary education until they were about eighteen years old. The boys and their parents chose for themselves which subjects they would study.

107

Mathematics, astronomy, public-speaking, philosophy, literature and music were popular. Physical education continued to play an important part and the boys could attend lessons given by a 'paidotribes' in a 'palaestra' (as in primary school) or else go along to a public sports-centre called a gymnasium. There were three of these in Athens, open to all citizens. As well as being used for sport, they often served as a centre for visiting professors giving lectures. Wealthy young men, anxious to further their education, could attend these lectures and discuss points of interest with the lecturers. Some lecturers, known as Sophists, gave talks in rich men's houses and took a few students for high fees. This can be seen as the equivalent of our University education.

At the age of eighteen, Athenian boys were registered in their parish, or 'deme', as 'Epheboi' (a word meaning 'young men'). They had to spend the next two years on military service before becoming full citizens of the city-state. They could then, if they wished, continue their education by attending more lectures in the gymnasia or by going along to one of the classes held by the Sophists.

Things to do:

Section A

Write in your jotter the heading *Schools and Education*. Underline. This will be the main heading. There will also be some sub-headings which you should copy neatly and underline.

1 GOING TO SCHOOL

Copy out this paragraph, filling in the blanks:

I went to my first school, ..., at .... years of age. An Athenian boy went to his first school at .... years of age. My parents take me to school or else I go with my friends. The Athenian boys were taken to school by .... This word actually means '.......-........' His duty was to .... Today both boys and girls go to school, but in Ancient Athens only the .... went to school. The .... stayed .... There, under the supervision of their ...., they learned to ....

2 EQUIPMENT AT SCHOOL

Again, copy out this paragraph, filling in the blanks.

In my class there are chairs and desks. In an Athenian school the boys had only .... There were no ....

I write in a ...., using a .... or a .... An Athenian boy had to use a .... and a .... to write with.

I have many books with covers and lots of pages. A Greek book was just ....
Draw and colour as many pieces of equipment as you have just mentioned which could have been found in an Athenian school.

3 SUBJECTS AT PRIMARY SCHOOL
Answer these question in sentences:
(a) What was a boy's first lesson at school?
(b) How did teachers try to make this task easier?
(c) Why was reading more difficult than it is today?
(d) Once a boy had learned to read, what was the next lesson?
(e) Why was this lesson considered so important?
(f) How much arithmetic did a boy learn in primary school?
(g) What is an abacus? Draw a diagram to explain how it works.
(h) Why was music important in Athenian education?
(i) Draw two musical instruments used by the Greeks. Label each drawing.
(j) Who was the 'paidotribes' and what did he teach?
(k) Name as many activities as you can which were practised by boys in the 'palaestra'.

4 SECONDARY EDUCATION
Copy out this short paragraph, filling in the blanks:
I finished primary school when I was .... years old. An Athenian boy probably finished his primary education at .... years. After primary school, I went to .... school; in Ancient Athens, after primary school, those boys whose parents were not rich .... Those with wealthy parents continued .... until they were about .... years old. The subjects they studied then were ....

5 HIGHER EDUCATION
Copy out this section, filling in the blanks:
Today, our main forms of Higher Education are ...., or .... In Athens a young man who wanted to continue his studies could attend .... in the .... and discuss points with the .... He could also go to .... given by the Sophists. These were men who ....

Section B
1 Using pieces of cardboard and Plasticine, make your own wax-tablet. Shape a piece of wood to make a stylus. You should be able to write on your tablet.

You could also make a miniature Greek book by rolling a long piece of paper into a scroll and attaching pieces of wood to each end. What must be done once you have got to the end of the book if the next reader is to be able to start immediately at the beginning?

2 'The School That I'd Like'. Write an essay on this subject, indicating what you would keep from the present system and what you would change.

3 The Greeks used to beat boys if they misbehaved. Today in Scotland pupils can be belted if they do wrong. Do you think this is right? What could be used in place of such corporal punishment? Perhaps a class debate could be staged on this topic.

People at work

Few people in Athens and the surrounding district were rich enough to lead a life of leisure, with no work to go to. There were many trades and occupations in Athens where free born citizens worked to make a living, alongside slaves and foreign workers. These foreign workers were called 'metics.' They performed a very important role in Athenian industry and often became rich and influential. They had to pay taxes and be registered as residents of the city, but they could never enjoy the full status of citizenship.

Although Athens was largely a city of industry and commerce, farming still played a large part in the life of the people. A large proportion of the inhabitants of Attica worked on the soil, and even within the city there were small plots and allotments. Most of the farms were small and worked by the farmer himself, with the help of several slaves. Extra help could be hired when necessary, as at harvest time.

The farmer's life was a hard one. The soil of Attica is not particularly rich and it needed constant and careful working if the crops were to be successful. To increase the area suitable for cultivation, hillsides were often terraced.

Farming methods were primitive. Some farmers ploughed their fields with teams of oxen and sowed corn. This was harvested early, some time between April and June. The corn was cut, as it had been for centuries, with a sickle. Threshing was done by oxen which moved round and round, trampling out the grain from the straw. The chaff was finally separated from the grain by tossing it into the air and letting the wind blow it away.

The farmers of Attica could never produce enough corn to

Terraced hillside in Crete

feed the whole population, and one of the Athenians' main imports was grain from overseas, mainly from Egypt and southern Russia.

Olives were grown widely in Attica, as they still are. The trees take a long time to grow to maturity, about sixteen years in all, and great care was needed to protect them from damage. The harvest of berries took place in late autumn. If the crop was particularly heavy, extra labour was hired to help out. The berries were placed in a press and crushed by a circular stone to produce the precious oil which had so many uses. Attica produced enough oil for her own needs and still had some left over to export to other countries.

Oxen ploughing *(above left)*

Wheat ripening in the sun *(top)*

Winnowing corn in modern Greece *(above)*

An olive grove

111

Vines also grow well in Attica, both on the plains and on the terraced hillsides. At harvest time the grapes were picked and carried to the wine-press. There, workers trod on the grapes and squeezed out the juice which ran into a special channel. It was then collected and stored in large jars, and allowed to ferment, by a natural process, into wine.

Treading grapes to make wine

Some farmers kept herds of livestock, mainly goats and sheep. These could survive easily on the rough, upland pastures which were unsuitable for cultivation.

Goats on a hillside

Within the city of Athens itself commerce and industry flourished. Much of the finance necessary for business transactions was provided by bankers. These bankers, who employed slaves to do much of the routine work, started off in business by acting as money-changers. They set up tables at the harbour or in the market-place, and exchanged foreign money into the local currency. Many of these money-changers prospered and were soon able to lend large sums of money at attractive rates of interest to cover the cost of a business-trip or the hire of a cargo-ship, or to insure a valuable cargo against loss at sea. It is interesting to note that the Ancient Greek word for table (at which these bankers sat) was 'trapeza' and that this word is still used in Modern Greek to mean 'a bank'.

The centre of commercial life in Athens was the Agora, or market place. Here, every morning, stalls were set up so that traders could sell their wares to the public. The country people flocked into the city to sell the produce of their farms at this market. All sorts of goods could be bought at the various stalls—items ranging from common foodstuffs to exotic perfumes. Stalls with similar products on sale were grouped together in the same part of the Agora.

Ancient Athens

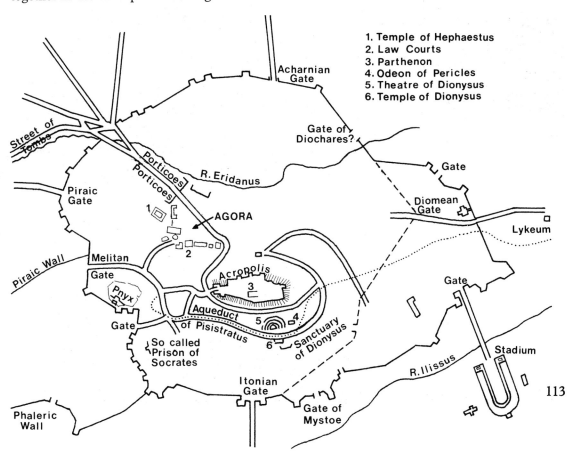

1. Temple of Hephaestus
2. Law Courts
3. Parthenon
4. Odeon of Pericles
5. Theatre of Dionysus
6. Temple of Dionysus

113

Barbers, fishmongers and bankers all worked on the north side. Barbers' shops were notorious as centres of gossip, as they often still are. Olive oil was sold on the east side. Books could be bought in the 'Orchestra' which was probably in the centre of the Agora. Free men and slaves could be hired out for work and gathered in the Agora, ready for inspection by prospective employers—free men were grouped together near the temple of Hephaestus; slaves were kept near the shrine of the Dioscuri, on the slopes of the Acropolis.

Many of the stalls were run by poor women who had to work for a living. These women were noted throughout the city for their coarse language! Weights and measures inspectors were used to check that the public were not cheated by unscrupulous stallholders, but there is an account of how some fishmongers used to wet their fish before placing it on the scale so that they could charge for the extra weight!

Market scene in the Agora

Round the Agora were placed all the important public buildings, including a council chamber, the army head-quarters, the law-courts, the mint where the silver coins were made, and a round building to house the official weights and measures. Although the market finished by mid-day, the Agora was still a busy place where people walked and talked, often about business, politics or even philosophy, under the colonnades (or 'stoa') which gave protection from the fierce sun.

'Professional' occupations were not as common in Ancient Athens as they are today. Politicians were mainly amateurs, elected for only a short spell. Government officials too were elected for a fixed (usually quite short) period. There were no lawyers, except the men who wrote speeches for delivery by a defendant in court. Teachers ran primary and secondary schools and could earn a moderate income from the fees they charged, though their status was never particularly high. Greek doctors were famous throughout the Ancient World and even today are recognized as the founders of modern medicine.

Industry in Athens was run on a small scale. There were no big factories, but just small workshops where free born Athenians, foreigners and slaves often worked together. A workshop with fifty men would have been considered big. These factories were of many types, making articles such as shoes, furniture, beds, arms, jewellery, pottery, statues and ironware. Often young apprentices worked alongside master craftsmen to learn a trade. Men of the same trade were very jealous of their skill and often banded together in associations or guilds to protect their interests. Usually all the followers of a particular trade lived and worked in the same part of the city.

Blacksmiths and metalworkers lived and worked together in that part of the city which lay near the temple of Hephaestos, their patron god. They used charcoal in their furnaces to build up sufficient heat for smelting the iron-ore into molten metal. This was then shaped by the blacksmiths into armour (helmets, swords, spearheads, shields), or simple utensils like pots and pans. In some factories bronze statues were made, as well as other items of artistic beauty—cups, goblets, jewellery.

Metalworkers

Sculptors and stonemasons formed another close-knit group of tradesmen. They worked near the blacksmiths at the temple of Hephaestos. There was always plenty of work for them to

115

Sculptors working on a statue

do in the city, especially in the time of Pericles when many new statues and temples were being built on the Acropolis. Athens was full of statues. Nearly every house, for religious reasons, had a statue of the god Hermes at the front door. The stonemasons were employed in the construction of the famous public buildings in the city. They cut, dressed and polished the stone slabs which had been delivered in a rough form from the quarries at Mt Pentelikos.

Perhaps the most important industry of all in Athens was that of pottery. All the potters lived in the same part of the city, a sort of 'Potters' Quarter', known as Cerameikos. To make the pots and vases which were so much a part of Athenian life, these craftsmen used clay which was found locally. The vases were shaped on a potter's wheel before being left to dry in the open air. Next, an artist decorated the vases either with scenes from mythology or from daily life. The vases were then fired at a high temperature in a well-ventilated kiln. At first, vases were produced with black silhouettes on a red-orange back-

Red Figure vase *(right)*

A potter at work

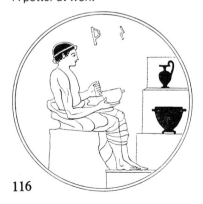

116

ground. Such vases are known as 'Black Figure' vases. Later it seemed more natural to keep the orange-red colours for the figures and to colour the background black. These later vases are called 'Red Figure' vases. Later still, other colours—blue, brown, pink—were added to make the scenes more attractive.

The Athenians, like other Greeks elsewhere, produced pots and vases of many different shapes for many different purposes —for wine, for water, for mixing wine and water, for holding grain, oil, perfume. The really large jars used for storing food were called 'amphorae'.

The pots and vases produced in Athens were admired throughout Greece, and were bought by merchants for export to many other cities and countries, some even beyond the bounds of the Greek world. The Etruscans, that mysterious people who lived in the north of Italy before the Romans, were greatly influenced by the work of the Greek potters and tried to copy their ideas.

Very many Greek pots and vases have been found by archaeologists. These experts often have to glue many broken pieces together, rather like a jig-saw puzzle, in order to restore the vase to its original shape. Hundreds of these vases can be seen today in museums throughout the world. From them we can see that the Greeks, and especially the Athenians, were a very skilful and artistic people. We can also learn, from the decorations on the vases, a great deal about the whole Greek way of life. Many of the illustrations in this book are taken from actual vase-paintings made over two thousand years ago by the people of Greece.

Black Figure vase

Amphorae found in the sea off the coast of North Africa

117

Things to do:

Section A

The main heading, to be placed at the top of the page, is *People at Work*. Several sub-headings will be used for each section. These should be copied and underlined.

1 FARMING

Copy out these sentences, filling in the blanks:

  (a) Farming played an .... part in the lives of the Athenian people.

  (b) Farmers produced ....

  (c) Their farming methods were ....

    Now write a short paragraph to explain sentence (c).

2 COMMERCE

Answer these questions in sentences:

  (a) What is the Modern Greek word for 'bank'?

  (b) Why is this word used with this meaning?

  (c) Why were bankers so important to the commercial life of Athens?

  (d) Where was the centre of commercial life in Athens? Write as vivid a description as possible of what could be seen every day in this place.

    Draw and colour a picture to illustrate your description.

3 THE PROFESSIONS

Make a list of all occupations today which are described as 'professions'. You may have to ask your teacher for help here.

  Which of the occupations you have listed could also be found in Ancient Athens?

4 INDUSTRY

  (a) Copy out this paragraph, filling in the blanks:

    Industry in Athens was run on a .... scale. Instead of big factories, the Athenians had only .... Some of the articles produced in Athens were .... To help with the work, ... were very often used. Normally, workers in the same trade joined together in a .... to .... This is similar to a .... today.

      Draw and colour a picture to illustrate this paragraph.

  (b) What sort of work was done by (i) blacksmiths; (ii) stonemasons and sculptors?

    Why was there plenty of work for stonemasons and sculptors in Athens at the time of Pericles?

  (c) (i) Where did the potters live and work?

    (ii) What does the English word 'ceramics' mean and how is it connected with Ancient Athens?

(iii) What did the potters use to make their vases?

(iv) What two colours were most commonly used on the vases?

(v) How were these two colours arranged in (1) the first vases; (2) later vases?

(vi) Look at the red-figure and black-figure vases printed on pp. 116 and 117. Draw both in your notebook and colour them in the correct way.

(vii) What different uses did the Greeks have for the pots and vases?

(viii) Why is the discovery of ancient pots and vases so important to modern archaeologists?

Section B

1 Make a Greek-style vase in clay or Plasticine.

2 An archaeologist faces a difficult task when he pieces together the fragments of a Greek vase. To see how difficult it can be, take an old cup with a pattern on it. Break it into small pieces and then try to glue it into one piece again.

Ships, Colonies and Trade

Ships

Greece is a very mountainous country so that travel by land is difficult. There are, however, many inlets of the sea which penetrate between the mountains. The common method of travel, therefore, was by sea and around Greece it has some pleasant features. There are neither tides nor currents and not much surf, and visibility for most of the year is excellent. Although the Greeks were great sailors, they still retained a fear of the sea during the winter and would only sail during the sailing season, which lasted from May to November. The Greek poet Hesiod says, 'when the Pleiades fall into the misty sea fleeing Orion's rude strength (the end of October or the beginning of November) then indeed gales of every kind rage. Then no longer sail on the sparkling sea.'

Merchant ships were built as strong as possible. They were heavy, wide and curved to hold bulky cargoes. They were driven by one sail rather than by oars. Merchant ships were, therefore, very slow but they travelled great distances.

Warships were built to be lighter and more streamlined than merchant ships and so they were faster. Penteconters were the early warships and they each had 50 oars (penteconta in Greek

Greek merchant ship

Yoon-Ah kim

means fifty). On a penteconter there was one bank of oars, 25 on each side.

A penteconter

There is some argument as to how triremes, the later Greek warships, were rowed. It may have been that the trireme was driven forward by a system involving three men to the one oar or there may have been a more complicated arrangement involving three oars. The three rowers must have been more or less on the one level, as the illustration shows.

How a trireme may have been rowed

Both the penteconter and the trireme had sails but these were not used in battle. At the prow of each there was a ramming device, usually shaped to look like some animal. The normal tactic in a battle was to gain a position facing the side of the enemy ship and to try to break the ship in two by ramming it fiercely.

The crews of merchant ships and warships were different. On the merchant ship the crew was made up of slaves but on the warship of citizens.

Colonies

The Greeks used ships not only around Greece but also to travel to the numerous colonies overseas. The great age of colonization was from about 750 BC down to about 550 BC and during this time over 600 colonies were established all over the Mediterranean Sea and the Black Sea.

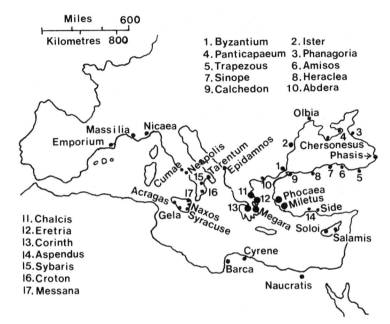

Greek colonies

The main reason for this colonization was too big a population in Greece. Round about 750 BC the birth rate started to increase and there simply was not enough space for all. Other reasons were lack of opportunity at home and sheer love of adventure.

A band of colonists was normally assisted by a mother city back in Greece. The mother city provided the leader of the expedition and organized it but it seems that many members often did not actually come from the particular mother city. This explains why the link between the colony and the mother city was not very strong. Once the colony had been established it became an independent city, being in no way under the power of the mother city. It would be built along the same pattern as the mother city and might have a special trading arrangement with it but that would be all.

The colonization had important results. First of all, with new cities being built, there was an increase in trade. Ships journeyed all over the Mediterranean Sea and the Black Sea. This increased trade benefited the cities involved and parti-

121

cularly the merchants, who carried out the trading. Some of these men gained tremendous personal wealth and importance and so they wanted political power. The result was that they presented a direct challenge to the old landowning nobles.

Trade

Money is very important in trading. The first currency of Greece was simply pieces of precious metals, mainly copper, bronze and silver. These pieces naturally had no set value and the only way to attach some sort of value to them was to weigh them. This was a very awkward way to carry on trade and eventually cities produced their own coins. These coins had a fixed weight, purity and value. By far the most common metal used in coinage was silver. The currencies of Athens and Corinth were the most important with regard to trade because these two cities were the greatest commercial forces. The coins had more or less the same names and values throughout the Greek cities: the obol, the drachma (worth six obols), the mina (worth 100 drachmas) and the talent (worth sixty minas). Where the cities differed was on the emblems put on the coins.

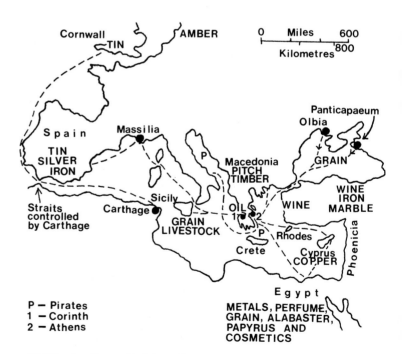

P — Pirates
1 — Corinth
2 — Athens

METALS, PERFUME,
GRAIN, ALABASTER,
PAPYRUS AND
COSMETICS

Principal trade routes

Merchants often sailed from Egypt to the Aegean by way of Cyprus or Phoenician ports, picking up slaves and Oriental luxury goods.

The main reason why the Greeks were such great traders was that a city simply could not supply all its needs. Opposite is a map illustrating the main trading routes and the goods found in particular places.

Athens was a prominent trading centre. The land of Attica was not suitable for the growing of grain and so the Athenians imported more than two thirds of the grain they required, mainly from Southern Russia. Another import essential to Athens was a ready supply of timber. This was for use in the building of ships, which maintained her power. Macedonia was the main supplier of timber. The Athenians would use cunning tricks to keep these goods coming to Athens. If, for example, a particular prince in a supply area proved to be awkward, they would even go so far as to promote a pretender to the throne. To pay for these imports the main Athenian exports were olive oil and beautiful pottery. This pottery was so well made that often it was bought more for its appearance than practical value.

Corinth was the other main trading city and her area of influence was the western coast of Greece along with Sicily and Southern Italy.

A trading deal was carried out as follows. A merchant borrowed a sum of money from a banker to purchase, for example, a cargo of grain from Southern Russia. The cargo itself was the only security. The merchant then made an arrangement with a ship-owner for space on a ship coming from Southern Russia back to Athens. When the ship arrived at Athens, buyers would bid for the grain in the market. Only at this time did the merchant know whether he had made a profit or a loss. It all depended on timing. If the merchant had estimated correctly that there was a real demand for grain, he could make a huge profit, but if he came back to find that there was plenty of cheap grain around, he might very well make a loss. He was obliged to pay the ship-owner his money but the banker took the loss along with the merchant.

Things to do:

1 Write one long sentence on each of the following:
   the Greek merchant ship; the penteconter; the trireme.
2 Two Greek colonies were Neapolis (the New City) in Southern Italy and **Massilia** in the south of the modern France. Try to discover, by looking at a modern map, what these cities are called today.
3 Give the reasons for the colonization.

4 Copy out the following, filling in the blanks:
.... obols are in a drachma;
.... drachmas are in a mina;
.... minas are in a talent.

5 Name the main imports and exports of Athens.

6 Make a drawing of a merchant ship, penteconter or trireme.

Slaves

Few of us today would approve of slave-labour with the cruelty and hardship it imposes upon our fellow human-beings. Yet all the peoples of the Ancient World, including the Greeks, had slaves. In some countries the slaves were very badly treated. The people of Ancient Athens, however, treated their slaves better than most other societies.

There were many slaves in Attica, the district of which Athens was the centre, probably about 125 000 in all. A large number of the slaves were prisoners of war. Some had been kidnapped by pirates or sold into slavery by poor parents. Others had been born to a slave mother and so became slaves themselves.

Greek and Phoenician traders carried all types of slaves from one end of the Mediterranean to the other. Every large city had its own slave-market. There you could find slaves of every age, condition, and nationality, both male and female.

Slaves from the Eastern Mediterranean were usually the most skilled and fetched high prices. Negro slaves were also expensive, not because of any skill, but because of their novelty value; often a wealthy man would buy a negro slave whose only duty would be to walk in front of him when he went out, thus ensuring a large, marvelling audience! Unskilled slaves who were nevertheless handsome or intelligent could also fetch good prices and usually found employment in private households. Pretty girls were popular buys and were used as dancers or musicians at feasts.

The lowest class of slaves came from the northern lands, people like the Thracians, or the Scythians from the icy plains of southern Russia. They were tall, strong and tough, and considered suitable only for hard, manual labour. In Athens, a selected group of Scythian archers was employed by the government to keep order within the city—a sort of police force. No doubt they were chosen for their formidable size and strength.

What kind of work did the slaves do? It has been estimated that in Attica 65 000 slaves were employed in private house-

A mug made in the form of a negro's head

A slave girl dancing

holds, fulfilling a variety of domestic duties. Women today buy machines to make the housework lighter; the Greek housewife, if her husband was rich, had slaves to do all the dull, routine jobs round the house. A wealthy family would also have a slave to act as a nurse for the young children. When the boys of the family started going to school, they were placed in the charge of an old, trusted slave called the 'paidagogos.' These household slaves, though legally the property of their masters, were treated kindly, often being regarded as members of the family. The instructions given by one Greek husband to his wife—'You will have to see that any servant who is ill is well cared for'—indicate the kind of treatment that many household slaves must have enjoyed.

Greek farmers likewise used slave-labour where today we use machinery. All the routine jobs of the farm—sowing, reaping, harvesting, shepherding, pruning vines, gathering olives, making wine—were carried out by slaves. The farm owner was thereby left free to devote his time to the overall management and successful running of the farm. Small farmers often had only one or two slaves and worked alongside them, treating them as fellow-workers rather than slaves.

Probably about 50 000 slaves worked in industry within the city of Athens. Most industries in Athens were small and consisted of an owner or employer, plus a few slaves. The father of Demosthenes employed about twenty-five slaves in his arms factory and about twenty in his bed-making factory. Sometimes the employer hired free men to work with his slaves. We hear of a citizen, employing two free Athenians and three slaves, who won a contract for fluting one temple column. It was not unknown for the slave owner to work alongside his slaves. The employment of slaves gave the master more time to devote to the management of his business, and allowed him, when necessary, to attend the meetings of the Ecclesia. These slaves employed in industry were allowed a considerable amount of freedom. In a shoemaking workshop, for example, a slave would come to work in the morning and obtain tools and materials from the owner. He then spent part of the day making shoes and the rest of the day selling them. He had to get the best price for his goods and paid over only a percentage to his master. The rest he kept for himself. He could easily save some of this money to buy his freedom, and then he could set himself up in business in his own right, perhaps with his own slaves.

The commercial world of Athens also depended heavily on slaves. The basic operations of merchants and traders were carried out by intelligent slaves who could read, write and

Slaves harvesting olives

A shoemaker at work

Inside a blacksmith's shop

count. These slaves were given every opportunity to improve their status and to gain their freedom. One such slave was Pasion, of Athens. He was owned by two bankers. He soon gained a reputation for hard work, honesty and intelligence. He became indispensable to the successful running of the business, and when the owners retired they turned everything over to him. He became one of the wealthiest and most influential businessmen in Athens, and eventually received the highest accolade possible: he was made a full citizen of Athens, a privilege normally reserved only for free-born Athenians.

In sharp contrast to such liberal treatment was the harsh reality of life in the silver mines at Laureion in the south of Attica. About 10 000 slaves worked in the mines: only the worst type of slave was sent there.

Conditions in the mines were unbelievably bad. The tunnels, or galleries, measured only 1×0.75 metres. This meant that the miners had to work on their hands and knees or lying flat on their backs. Ventilation was poor and the temperature extremely high. Choking dust was everywhere. The roof might collapse at any moment. The slaves worked long, hard hours— at least ten hours without a break. They had no prospects of ever being released. Hardly ever seeing the sun, they worked in semi-darkness until they dropped. It was a living death, often mercifully short.

Conditions in the silver mines at Laureion represent one of the few serious blots on the Athenian record as regards the treatment of slaves. Another disgraceful feature was that no slave could give evidence in a court of law unless he was tortured first. Only then would a slave tell the truth. Some individual slave owners were no doubt cruel: such is human nature. 'Treat the slave as you like,' says a character in one of Aristophanes' plays,' put hot bricks on him, pour acid down his nose, put him on the rack, whip him, use the cat-o'nine-tails.' We may allow for some comic exaggeration in these lines—life could not always have been so bad. In general, the Athenians treated their slaves well. They realized that slaves worked better if well looked after. They regarded many of their slaves as fellow men who could help them obtain a higher standard of living. The well-being of the Athenian economy depended largely on the successful co-operation of slave and master. One ancient account of the time, written by someone who did not really approve of the Athenian way of life, sums it all up neatly:

> Slaves are extremely undisciplined at Athens. You are not allowed to hit them, and a slave will not get out of your way. I will tell you why. If it were allowed . . . one might easily strike an Athenian by mistake for a slave; they are no better dressed and no better in appearance. . . . And if you wonder at their letting the slaves be comfortable, and some of them indeed have quite a high standard of living, there is sense in that too. Where sea-power is important, it is necessary that slaves should work for money, so that we may collect revenue from them, and we must let them be free. . . .

Things to do:

Section A

1 The heading is quite simply *Slaves*. Answer these question in sentences:
   (a) How many slaves were there in Attica?
   (b) How did someone become a slave in Ancient Greece?
   (c) Where did a Greek go to buy a slave?
   (d) Which type of slave fetched (a) a high price; (b) a low price?
   (e) What sort of work did a slave do in a private household?
   (f) What sort of work did a slave do on a farm?
   (g) Describe the work and condition of slaves in industry.
   (h) What could a slave-owner do with the spare time caused by slaves doing all the routine work?
   (i) Why was Pasion a remarkable slave?
   (j) Which slaves suffered the worst treatment? Describe their work and their working conditions.

127

(k) In general, how did the Greeks treat their slaves? Quote evidence from an original Greek source to support your answer.

Section B

1 Draw and colour a picture to illustrate what you imagine the life of a slave in *either* industry *or* mining was like.

2 Compose/design a newspaper advertisement for a slave-market.

3 Compose a conversation between an Ancient Athenian defending slavery and a modern person attacking the idea of keeping slaves.

4 Imagine that you are a slave in the mines. Write an account of your life.

5 Follow-up study: find out about the slave-trade in the eighteenth/nineteenth centuries; about William Wilberforce; about the US Civil War; about Abraham Lincoln.

6 Think about this question and discuss it with your teacher and your friends: has slavery really been abolished?

Law and the Law Courts

Police

In ancient Athens there was no police force such as we have nowadays. The Athenians did not like the idea of one citizen acting as policeman over another and so they used slaves to help them to keep order in the city. The slaves who were used for this purpose were tribesmen from the north, Scythian archers clad in their native trousers and high-peaked caps, who lived in tents not far from the Acropolis. Their duties did not involve the pursuit of criminals nor the detection of crime. They were used mostly for crowd control in the assembly and the law courts.

Laws

The first man to write down a code of laws for the Athenians is said to have been Draco. The punishments which he fixed were so cruel that people said that Draco's laws were written in blood. He himself declared that even the less serious crimes deserved the penalty of death and that he could think of no greater punishment for worse crimes. Some time later, in 594 BC, a wise man named Solon wrote new laws which were so fair that they were not changed for many years.

A Scythian archer stringing his bow

Law courts

People who committed any crime, whether petty theft or high treason would be tried in court by their fellow citizens. However, cases which involved murder were tried before a special court of old men which met in the open air on the Areopagus or 'Hill of Mars'.

The Areopagus looking east towards the Acropolis

There was no public prosecutor in Athens. Instead it was left to individual citizens to accuse any person who had done wrong. To make sure that one citizen would not accuse another for reasons of spite or malice, the accuser would be punished by a fine if he failed to win at least one-fifth of the total number of votes cast by the jury. The accuser first of all served a summons on the offender in the presence of witnesses. Later on they both appeared before a magistrate and evidence was written down by a clerk. Some time later the case would come up before a jury.

A court scene

129

Each of the ten tribes in Attica had to produce a list of 600 citizens, men over thirty years of age and of good standing, who would serve as jurymen. These men were divided into groups who would try cases in the courts. No one knew until the day of the trial who would serve as jurymen for any particular case, so that bribery would be almost impossible. Jurymen were paid a small fee for their services and so even poorer citizens could afford to take part. The size of juries was much larger than nowadays, numbering 201 or 401 or sometimes even more. These were the people who decided if the accused man was guilty and, if so, what punishment he should receive. Unlike the judge who presides over our courts nowadays the magistrate who presided over the Athenian court—they called him the Archon—did not have the power to decide the penalty.

Voting pebbles as used by jurors. Solid hubs meant not guilty, hollow ones guilty

The comic playwright, Aristophanes, poked fun at elderly Athenian men who were too fond of sitting on juries and judging their fellow citizens.

> The master has jury-mania, worse than anyone ever; he is hooked on jury-service; he moans unless he is sitting in the front row of the jury. At night he doesn't get a wink of sleep; or if he dozes for a second he is dreaming of the water-clock; he is so used to holding the voting pebble that he wakes up gripping his thumb and two fingers tightly together. . . . He hurries before daybreak to the court house and sleeps there clinging like a limpet to the doorpost.

On the day of the trial the accuser and the accused each made a long speech, a time-limit being set for each speaker by a water-clock. Each of them was expected to speak on his own behalf, although they might get professional speech writers to make up their speeches which they would then learn off by heart. They used arguments which would not be allowed in a court of law today. They tried to win the pity of the jury and sometimes an accused man might even bring his wife and children into the court dressed in rags so that people would feel sorry for him. Neither side called witnesses, except to swear that the statements they had previously made before the magistrate were true. There was no cross-examination. After the speeches came the verdict. There were two jars, one marked

A water-clock

'guilty', the other 'not guilty'. Each juror had a pebble which he placed in one or other of the two jars. If the verdict was 'guilty', the penalty had to be decided. If there was no fixed penalty for the crime the prosecutor would propose a penalty and the defendant had the right to propose a different punishment. This was a sensible enough practice as the accused person was likely in his own interests to propose something which the jury would accept.

The penalties under Athenian law varied between fines, exile and death. The Athenians had no jails suitable for detaining prisoners for a long time.

A famous trial

A famous trial took place in a court in Athens in the spring of the year 399 BC. The accused was Socrates. He had spent a great part of his life going around questioning people about the meaning of goodness, or justice, or courage, or discussing the evidence for the existence of the gods, or whether people can be taught to be good, or how to make the city great. He tried in this way to get people to think for themselves, and he often showed that the beliefs which they had held all their lives were without foundation. Some of the young men who had been his followers had turned out to be a disappointment to their families, seeming to have no respect for man or god. There were people who felt that Socrates and his teachings were to blame. Now at the age of seventy Socrates found himself on trial for his life before a jury of 501 of his fellow citizens. The charges against him were that he had been leading young citizens astray and had been teaching them not to pay attention to the gods of the city.

It was, Socrates maintained, completely untrue to suggest that he was an atheist or that he taught others to be atheists. Indeed it was God who ordered him to search for the truth, and he would not cease to fulfil the command of God even if he had to die for his belief.

Jurors' tickets assigning them to a case

> Men of Athens, I have the warmest affection for you: but I shall obey God rather than you, and while I have life and strength I shall never cease my quest for truth, saying, as I always do, to anyone I meet:
> 'You, my friend—a citizen of the great and mighty and wise city of Athens—are you not ashamed of devoting yourself to acquiring the greatest amount of money and honour and reputation and caring so little about wisdom and truth and the greatest improvement of your soul?' And if the person

131

with whom I am arguing says "Yes, but I do care"; then I do not leave him or let him go at once but I shall interrogate and examine and cross-examine him, and if I find that he has no virtue in him, but only says that he has, I shall rebuke him for scorning the things that are of most importance and caring more for what is of less worth.'

Referring to the accusation that he had led the young men of Athens astray, he pointed out that many of the relatives of these young men were in court. None of these had come forward to accuse him, but in fact were all present to support him.

Socrates ended his speech by explaining why he did not follow the practice, usual at Athens, by which defendants brought their family into court in order to appeal to the feelings of the jury. He did not think that such an action would be right for him in view of his age and what people thought of him.

People think Socrates is somehow superior to most men. I have seen men who are quite well thought of, behaving as if being put to death would be terrible: as if they would go on living for ever if you didn't kill them!

But anyway, I think it is not right to try to move a juryman's feelings. He is here to judge, not to be kindhearted.

If he tried to get the jury to break their oaths, he went on, he would be teaching them to disbelieve the gods.

For I do believe that there are gods, and to you and to God I entrust my case to decide it as shall be best for me and for you.

Jurymen voting

The jurymen were now called upon to cast their votes. Socrates was found guilty by a majority of fifty-nine. The penalty called for by the prosecution was death, but by Athenian law Socrates was allowed to suggest an alternative punishment. He told the jury that all that he had done was for the benefit of Athens and so he thought that what he deserved was to be entertained in the Town Hall like a victor at the Olympic Games. Urged by his friends, however, he agreed to the proposal of a fine.

The jury voted once more. The sentence was death.

Things to do:

Section A

1 Write down the heading *The Laws of Athens*. Underline it. Then answer in sentences the following questions:

(a) What did people mean when they said that Draco's laws were 'written in blood'?

(b) Nowadays what do we mean when we describe a law as 'Draconian'?

(c) Name the man who wrote new and just laws to take the place of Draco's laws.

2 Write down the heading *The Law Courts*. Underline it.

(a) Write down two ways in which an Athenian jury differed from a jury nowadays.

(b) How did the Athenians try to ensure that no one could bribe a juryman?

(c) Explain in detail the steps which an Athenian citizen would take if he wished to bring another citizen to trial for committing a crime.

(d) If a defendant was found guilty how was his punishment decided?

Section B

1 Arrange a trial in your classroom. Appoint an archon to preside over the court. The accuser and the accused should have their speeches prepared beforehand. The rest of the class will form the jury and will vote for the verdict and, if necessary, decide the punishment.

Death and Funerals

The Greeks believed in a life after death, but this life was a pale shadow of life on earth and not something to look forward to. When someone died, his body was laid out with a coin in its mouth—the fare for the old boatman, Charon, who ferried the souls of the dead across the River Styx into the Underworld. The mourners all wore black and cut their hair short, giving the clippings as an offering to the dead. A honey cake was offered to Hades, the god of the Underworld. Sad, mournful songs were sung by the relatives of the dead man.

At the funeral the body was placed on a bier. This was carried on the shoulders of friends as they made their way to the cemetery. A wealthy family might hire mourners to make the funeral procession seem grander. Flute-players led the way. Sometimes the body was buried; more often it was cremated. The ashes were collected and placed in a vase or urn which was usually beautifully decorated. The ashes were then buried along with some of the dead man's possessions which might be useful in the after-life. When this had been done, a feast was held, attended by all the mourners.

Skeleton with a coin in the mouth

One of the worst fates that could happen to a Greek was not to be buried properly. This meant that his soul would wander the earth, an unhappy spirit. Antigone, in the famous Greek legend, risked her life to give her dead brother the correct funeral rites. Greek sailors who might be drowned at sea with no relatives to lay out the body and place the coin in the mouth, tried to safeguard their passage to the Underworld by carrying a piece of gold in their ear as the fare for Charon. Could this be the origin of the single earring often worn by later sailors and pirates?

At the funeral of an important person, a friend might make a speech, praising the dead man. One such speech has been preserved for us by the Greek historian, Thucydides. He records the words which Pericles is supposed to have used at the funeral of the Athenian soldiers killed fighting in the Peloponnesian War against Sparta. Here is part of that famous speech:

> They gave their lives to the city, and to all of us, and for their own selves they won praises that never grow old, the most splendid of sepulchres—not the sepulchre in which their bodies are laid but where their glory remains eternal in men's minds, always there on the right occasion to stir others to speech or to action. For famous men have the whole earth as their memorial: it is not only the inscriptions on their graves in their own country that mark them out; no, in foreign lands also, not in any visible form but in people's hearts, their memory abides and grows.

The graves of the dead were always marked with some kind of stone. Sometimes it was just a plain slab of marble, with a simple decoration and a brief inscription like this:

> Amphicares, father of the dead youth, mourning a fine son, erected this stone to Chairedemos. Phaidimos made it.

Some stones were more elaborate and portrayed the dead person as he or she was when alive and enjoying life. The photograph shows a woman examining her jewel-box and admiring its contents. Another stone in the British Museum shows a man riding on horseback with a boy running behind him. The inscription on the stone says:

> After enjoying many pleasant sports with my companions, I who sprang from earth am earth once more. I am Aristocles, of Peiraeus, son of Menon.

One Greek poet, Simonides of Ceos, was very well known for the inscriptions he composed for tomb-stones. Perhaps his most famous inscription, or epitaph as they are called, was for the Spartans who fell at Thermopylae fighting against the Persians:

Bear word to Sparta, Stranger passing by,
That here, obedient to her word, we lie.

Things to do:

Section A

1   The heading is *Death and Funerals*
    Below is a skeleton (!) summary of this topic. Expand it into a full piece of information with two or three paragraphs.
    Life after death — coin in mouth — Charon — black clothes — hair clippings — sad songs — bier — cemetery — burial or cremation — feast — speech — grave-stones — epitaphs.

Section B

1   Compose *either* a funeral speech for soldiers who died fighting for this country in the last war, *or* an epitaph to be inscribed on their tomb.

The inscription at Thermopylae

135

11 The Greek Thinkers- Mind and Matter

Medicine

Before the sixth century BC the treatment of disease was in the hands of priests of Asclepius, the God of healing, and they held the idea that illnesses were sent by the Gods and that they were something divine. However, by the end of the fifth century BC a new approach to medicine had been set up largely due to the research carried out by a man who has been called 'the father of modern medicine'. This famous man, named Hippocrates, was born on the island of Cos (just off modern Turkey) about the year 460 BC. He led a wandering life, always, however, returning to his birth-place on the island of Cos to supervise a school of medicine which he established there.

Hippocrates believed that diseases had a 'natural' cause and that treatment should be based on 'observed' fact, not left to the whim of some God as had previously been believed. His followers carefully observed and recorded illnesses of their patients so that they might be able to forecast the course of the sickness and treatment then varied according to observation. Their method was a scientific or modern approach to sickness. One record of illness runs as follows:

The young man who was lying ill at the Liars market took a fever after running and unusual physical exertion.

Day 1 Bowel upset, many thin bilious motions; urine thin, rather black; no sleep, thirsty.

Day 2 All symptoms worse; excretions more unfavourable; no sleep; mental processes deranged, slight sweating.

Day 3 Uncomfortable, thirsty, nausea, much tossing about in distress, wandering in mind; extremities livid and cold; hypochondrium on both sides strained and rather flabby.

Day 4 No sleep; a turn for the worse.

Day 5 Died.

Hippocrates—the father of modern medicine

What this young man was suffering from was probably typhoid fever and although death was the result, the important fact is that it was studied closely in attempt to understand the natural cause for the illness and its course with the aim in mind to bring about some cure.

Hippocrates gave the lead in this respect by his work on quinsy, epilepsy, tapeworm and many other diseases. He is supposed to have left behind six books on the diagnosis and treatment of disease. It is to Hippocrates that the Doctor's oath is ascribed which attempted to make medicine an honest and respectable profession, and this oath still governs much of the attitude of medicine even today. It runs as follows:

I swear by Apollo . . . to reckon him who taught me this art equally dear to me as my parents. . . . I will impart a knowledge of the art to my own sons, and those of my teachers. . . . I will give no deadly medicine to any one if asked nor suggest any such counsel. . . . Into whatever houses I enter, I will go into them for the benefit of the sick, and will abstain from every voluntary act of mischief. . . . Whatever . . . I see or hear, in the life of men . . . I will not divulge. . . .

Since the Greeks were always involved in war, the demand for surgery and amputation was common and surgeons had plenty of practice on the battlefield. As a result they were capable of removing parts of the skull to remove pressure in cases of fracture and could treat fractured or dislocated limbs. When operating, however, they were handicapped by lack of anaesthetics which meant that the operation had to be performed quickly and the knife used boldly to prevent death by shock.

Anatomy could not be studied so much in detail because cremation of the dead prevented observation and it was not until later on when many Greeks settled in Egypt that dissection of corpses was practised.

The value of dissection of the human body was demonstrated by two doctors who came from Alexandria in Egypt—Herophilus and Erasistratus. The really important part of their work was to explain how the brain worked and the nervous system attached to it. They were able to establish the connection between the brain and the nerves and the difference between sensory and motor nerves. It was these two men who finally solved what the grey matter of the brain was, thereby creating the new science of physiology. Herophilus did a lot of work on the arteries and the heart which he knew caused the pulsation in the body which eventually lead to the discovery of the circulation of the blood.

First-aid on the battlefield

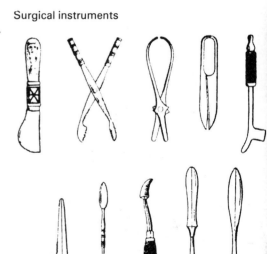

Surgical instruments

However, again and again in the writings of the Hippocratic school of medicine we come upon constant references to the need for careful and accurate observation. In one of his books Hippocrates describes the symptoms of many diseases as they were learned from countless observations and if some of them seem too simple for us they were not in the fifth century BC. Some of these are as follows:

1 Tuberculosis occurs chiefly between the ages of eighteen and thirty-five.
2 When sleep puts an end to delirium it is a good sign.
3 Old men endure fasting more easily than middle-aged men, youths endure fasting badly and worst of all children especially those with an unusual vitality.
4 The old generally have fewer complaints than the young, but when they have chronic diseases, they usually end fatally.
5 If a convalescent eats well, but fails to put on weight it is a very bad sign.
6 If there is no swelling after severe and grave wounds it is a very bad sign.
7 Do not disturb a patient either during or just after a crisis and do not attempt experiments with purges or diuretics.
8 We must attend to the appearance of the eyes in sleep as seen from below; for if a portion of the white can be seen between the closing eyelids and if this is not connected with diarrhoea or severe purging then it is a bad and fatal sign.

So with patience and increasing ability to recognize symptoms the ancient Greeks received treatment as good as any until the eighteenth century AD.

'Life is short and the art is long,' wrote Hippocrates adding sorrowfully: 'the opportunities are fleeting, experiments are dangerous and judgement is always difficult.'

Things to do:

1 Make drawings of early surgical instruments.
2 What does the word 'anaesthetic' mean? Why is this so important to medicine?
3 How did the work of Hippocrates differ from doctors before his time?
4 What does the word 'symptom' mean in medicine? Why is it so important?
5 What handicaps did Hippocrates have in his efforts to treat patients?

6　What big difference do you see between treatment of illness in Ancient Greece and treatment that is given today?
7　Do doctors today still take the Hippocratic oath?
8　How much do doctors today still keep to the ideas that are mentioned in the Hippocratic oath?
9　Draw either (a) first aid on the battlefield; *or* (b) the doctor's surgery.

Science

When does an interest in Science begin? It grows out of a sense of wonder—'my goodness, so that's how it works?'. This sense of wonder did not really take hold of the Greeks until they came into contact with the Babylonians and Egyptians from whom they learned new ideas about mathematics and astronomy. The Greeks were fascinated by these new ideas and soon they themselves began to ask questions about everything around them.

Geography

The first 'world' map

Hecataeus of Miletus (550–476 BC) was the first geographer of any importance who tried to form a full picture of what the world looked like. He travelled throughout the Mediterranean Sea, the Persian Empire, Egypt and Africa collecting scraps of information from sailors and merchants. He examined all this information carefully and published it together with a map of the world.

The world according to Hecataeus

The land for Hecataeus was completely surrounded by water which he named 'Ocean'. The River Nile was connected to this 'Ocean'. The land itself was in the centre, round-shaped and cut into two halves by the Mediterranean Sea, Black Sea, and Caspian Sea.

About 30 years after Hecataeus died, his ideas were challenged by Herodotus, who certainly asked the right questions although he could not always supply the right answers.

The yearly flooding of the River Nile

'When the River Nile overflows,' says Herodotus, 'it floods both its banks to an average distance of forty miles. I would particularly like to know why it starts flooding in the middle of summer and continues for three months. This is exactly the

1.	Caspian Sea.	7.	Black Sea.
2.	Persian Gulf.	8.	R. Borysthenes
3.	R. Euphrates.	9.	R. Tanais.
4.	R. Tigris.	10.	R. Phasis.
5.	Carthage.		
6.	Pillars of Hercules.		

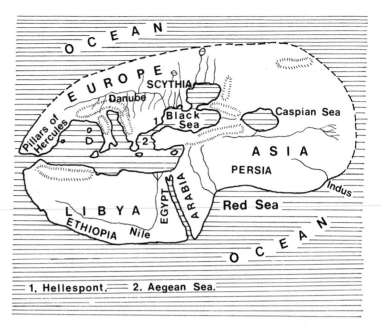

The world according to Herodotus

opposite of what any normal river does, and no one in Egypt knows why it happens.'

Herodotus dismissed the explanation which Hecataeus gave as something out of a children's story-book. Hecataeus suggested that 'there is a river called Ocean which is the whole reason for the Nile rising as it does because it flows out of the River Ocean'. There were two other theories about this strange flooding of the Nile which Herodotus rejected. The first one was that every summer winds blew from the north for forty days which prevented the Nile from flowing normally to the sea. The second was that it was caused by snow falling in the mountains of Libya. This last explanation, which Herodotus could not accept came very near the truth, given later by Aristotle when he said that the flooding was caused by tropical rains falling in the highlands of Africa during the spring and summer.

The course of the River Nile

Herodotus was right in assuming that the River Nile rose somewhere inland, but the course he determined for it was inaccurate. 'The course of the River Nile,' says Herodotus, 'is known for a considerable distance beyond Egypt, in fact, for about one thousand miles. Beyond this no one can say very much for certain since the land is sun-baked desert.' He thought it was the same length as the River Danube and parallel to it.

Phoenicians sail round Africa

Herodotus did not know much about the southern part of Africa, but his description of it reveals that sailors had certainly sailed round its whole coastline.

> The south of Libya (Africa) is no mystery. It is completely surrounded by water, except where it borders on Asia. The Egyptian king sent off some ships manned by Phoenicians. He ordered them to sail right round the coast until they reached the Mediterranean through the Pillars of Hercules, and so come back again to Egypt. Starting from the Red Sea the Phoenicians sailed along the sea which lies near Libya. Each autumn they stayed on land, sowed crops and waited to harvest them. Then they set sail again. After voyaging like this for two years, they sailed round the Pillars of Hercules and reached Egypt. One thing they reported was that while they were sailing round the south of Libya, they had the sun on their right.

Herodotus did not know about the relationship between the sun and the equator, but this fact about the sailors having the sun on their right while sailing west is proof that they did in fact sail right round Africa.

The size of Asia and Europe

Herodotus also questioned quite accurately the idea which Hecataeus had about the land on the earth being packed into a neat little ball. He was aware that there was still more land in Asia to be explored, although he did not know much of what lay beyond the River Indus, and his knowledge of Europe was limited:

> I cannot speak accurately about the farthest western parts of Europe. I do not believe that there is a River Eridanus (River Elbe) flowing into the Northern Sea from where our amber comes, nor have I any knowledge of the Tin Islands (Cornwall) from where we get our tin.

Northern Europe, to which Herodotus refers, had to wait another century before it was explored by Pytheas who came from Marseilles (originally a Greek colony).

Pytheas sails round Britain

Pytheas was a scientific navigator; he was able to calculate the latitude of Marseilles exactly and was one of the first Greeks to

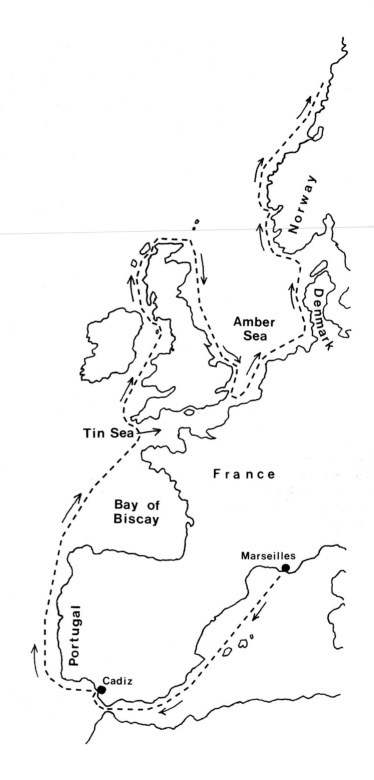

The voyage of Pytheas

establish a connection between the moon and the tides. Pytheas and his companions set sail from Marseilles between 328 and 321 BC. They passed through the Pillars of Hercules, visited Cadiz and then sailed north along the coasts of Portugal and France. They were aware of the great depth of the Bay of Biscay. From this part onwards, Pytheas was in unknown territory. He entered a new sea which he named the 'Tin Sea' (English Channel). He noted the islands and the names of the peoples. He landed on what he named the 'Land of Tin' (Cornwall) where he heard stories about the rest of the island. So for six weeks (in April and May) he sailed up the Western shores of Britain right up to Cape Wrath in the North of Scotland. He disembarked several times to measure the height of the tides and to make observations about the people. Britain, as Pytheas describes it, was an island, large and triangular and bigger than Sicily. Pytheas then sailed right round the North of Scotland, down the East coast to Kent. After this he sailed eastwards across 'The Amber Sea' (North Sea) to 'The Amber Isles' (Frisian Isles and Heligoland) where he discovered the River Eridanus (River Elbe) which Herodotus mentioned. Pytheas remained in the 'Amber Isles' during May and June collecting samples of the yellow amber. Pushing north he sailed past Jutland, up the Skagerrak to Thule (Norway) where he travelled about. He describes accurately a 'Fjord', the Gulf-Stream, and the long days of twenty-one or twenty-two hours. He attempted to sail further north, but had to turn back because 'the sea was neither water anymore, nor air'. What he had reached was the Great Ice Barrier in the Arctic Circle. He returned to Marseilles in October after a voyage of eight months where he wrote about his voyage and observations in his book *About the Ocean*.

Other explorers

While Pytheas was penetrating into the seas round Northern Europe, there was a fever for discovery and adventure else-where. Euthydemus from Marseilles sailed down the coast of Africa to Senegal. Hippalus sailed from the Red Sea to the coast of Malabar in southern India using the monsoon wind instead of sailing close to the shore. After this, merchants sailed from the Red Sea in July and sailed back from India in December. The single journey took twenty days. Eudoxus from Cyzicus sailed through the Mediterranean, out through the Pillars of Hercules and then right round Africa. The courage of these explorers knew no limits.

Things to do:

Section A
1 Copy the map of Hecataeus.
2 Copy the map of Herodotus.
3 What changes or alterations did Herodotus make in his map compared with the one of Hecataeus?

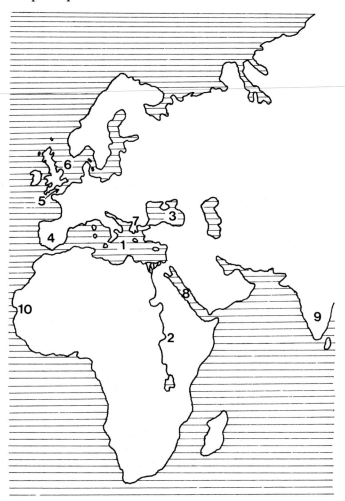

4 Above there is a blank map with numbers on it. Write down in your jotter the number and what it represents.
   e.g. 1   Mediterranean Sea
5 Copy the map showing the voyage of Pytheas.

Section B
1 Was the continent of America also known to the ancient peoples? Find out more by reading about Thor Heyerdahl.

Astronomy

What shape is the earth? Why does the moon change its shape?
Is the sun or the earth the centre of the universe? What does
the circumference of the earth measure? How long does it take
the moon to go round the earth? How long does it take the
earth to go round the sun? These were the sort of questions
which Greek astronomers tried to answer.

What shape is the earth?

In the sixth century BC Greek astronomers knew that the earth
was round. They realized that the earth's shadow caused
eclipses of the moon and saw that it was the shadow of something
round.

Why does the moon change its shape?

Anaxagoras (500–428 BC) was able to explain this. The moon,
he said, circled round the earth. According to its position in
this circuit round the earth we saw more or less of the moon
because of the light it reflected from the sun. Using this idea
Anaxagoras was able to explain what caused an eclipse of the
moon.

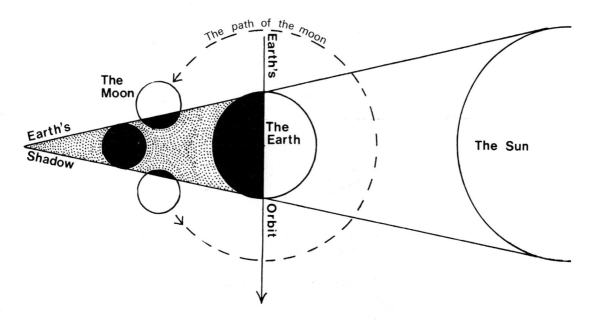

Is the sun or the earth the centre of the universe?

Nearly all Greek astronomers put the earth in the centre of the universe with all the other planets revolving around it.

Aristarchus of Samos (310–230 BC) rejected this idea and put the sun in the centre. 'The sun,' said Aristarchus, 'is much larger than the earth, 300 times larger' (it is in fact 1 300 000 times larger). It seemed strange to Aristarchus that the larger sun should revolve round the smaller earth. From this he formed the conclusion 'the earth is a planet which revolves about the sun like the other planets completing its revolution in one year'. Since Aristarchus also believed that the earth turned on itself in a day as it went round the sun, he was able to explain why day followed night and why we have the seasons of the year. Aristarchus was laughed at for his ideas and he was unable to convince others because he had no advanced equipment to prove his theory.

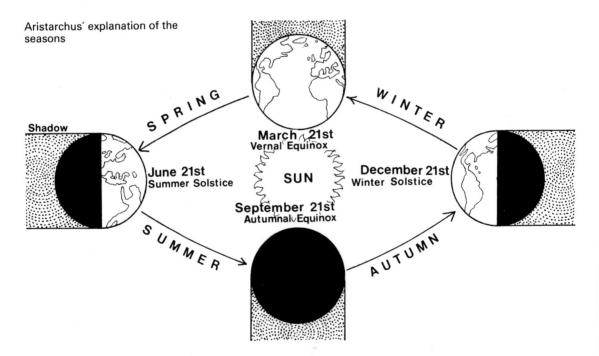

Aristarchus' explanation of the seasons

What does the circumference of the earth measure?

While Eratosthenes of Cyrene (275–195 BC) was attempting to improve upon the map of the earth by constructing a network of lines of latitude and longitude, he discovered a very simple but ingenious way of measuring the earth's circumference.

At Alexandria, as elsewhere in Egypt, there was a gnomon which was used for marking out land again after the River Nile flooded every year. Eratosthenes used this gnomon in his calculation.

Eratosthenes knew that 800 kilometres away from Alexandria there was the famous well at Syene. On mid-summer day the sun was directly above this well and so the sun's rays would go right down this well and continue to the centre of the earth. Knowing this fact, Eratosthenes measured at the same time of day the angle which the shadow of the gnomon made with the sun's rays. This angle was 7°. Since the sun's rays are parallel the angle at the centre of the earth between Alexandria and Syene was also 7°. The arithmetic after this was as follows:

$7° = \frac{1}{50}$ of $360°$ (i.e. $\frac{1}{50}$ of a circle).

∴ 800 kilometres $= \frac{1}{50}$ of the circumference of the earth.

∴ 800×50 kilometres $=$ the circumference of the earth.

∴ 40 000 kilometres $=$ the circumference of the earth.

Eratosthenes was more or less correct.

However, he made two mistakes in his calculation which cancelled each other out. Alexandria and Syene are not exactly in the same line of longitude, and the distance 800 kilometres is not accurate. Nevertheless his method was very scientific.

How long does it take the moon to go round the earth?

Hipparchus, who did research in Alexandria between 161 and 127 BC, calculated the time it took the moon to go round the earth to be 29 days, 12 hours, 44 minutes and 2·5 seconds, which is less than one second of an error.

He also calculated the time it took the earth to go round the sun as to be 365 days, 5 hours, 55 minutes and 12 seconds which is 6 minutes and 26 seconds in excess. Hipparchus observed the formation of a new star or 'Nova' which Chinese astronomers working at the same time dated as 134 BC. Hipparchus also produced his 'star catalogue' which was almost a complete record of eight hundred and fifty stars. After Hipparchus, astronomy suffered a setback owing to a new interest that was developing for astrology and virtually nothing new was discovered.

A gnomon (Cleopatra's Needle) similar to the one used by Eratosthenes

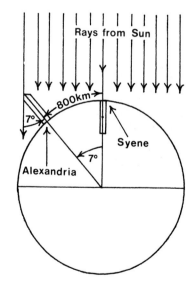

Eratosthenes' calculation

Things to do:

Section A

1 Make a list of the facts accepted today about astronomy which were discovered by the Greeks.

1 Why were the Greeks so interested in astronomy?
2 What value is there in studying astronomy?

Biology and Botany

Biology (the study of living things)

The 'father' of biology was Aristotle (384–322 BC), the son of a doctor. It was probably his father who first awakened in him a love for animals and nature, but unfortunately his father died when he was still young. Why he was so enthusiastic about studying living things, Aristotle explains himself:

> Every part of nature is marvellous, and we should try to study every kind of animal without being put off in any way, because each one of them will reveal to us something natural and beautiful. If any person thinks that the examination of the rest of the animal kingdom is an unworthy task, then he should also consider it not worthwhile studying man. For no one can look at the simple parts of the human being—blood, flesh, bones, vessels and such—without being a little upset.

Aristotle wrote books on many other subjects, but nothing was closer to his heart, or held a larger part in his life than the study of living things. It accounts for about one-third of all the books he wrote. The task which Aristotle set himself was almost an impossible one—to catalogue every living thing. Naturally, this attempt was too gigantic to be accomplished without some mistakes, and they number only about a dozen serious ones out of thousands of observations. He maintained quite wrongly that women have fewer teeth than men; that a man has only eight pairs of ribs; that arteries are full of air; that the brain is cold; and that a person has only one lung.

Despite these serious errors the rest of his research was very conscientious and surprisingly accurate if we appreciate the fact that he had no microscope and only the sharpness of his own eyes to rely on.

He investigated in great detail the circulatory system of animals, their lungs, heart, and blood vessels. When studying birds, he was particularly interested in the embryo or the early development of life within the egg. The following is his account of the development of the embryo of the common hen. Day after day he watched closely. On the fourth day he saw a red speck appear in the white, and the speck began to beat like a heart—it was a heart, the heart of the unborn chick.

The following words are Aristotle's:

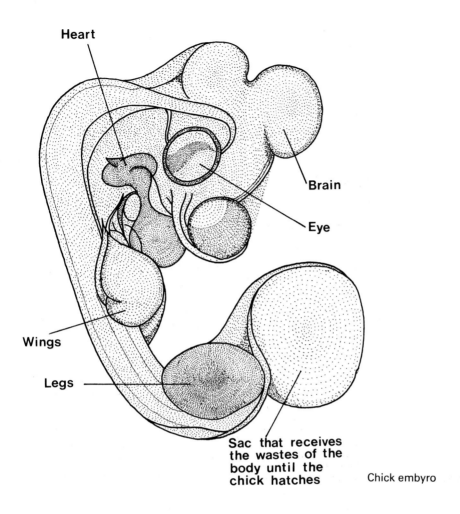

Heart

Brain

Eye

Wings

Legs

Sac that receives
the wastes of the
body until the
chick hatches

Chick embyro

With the common hen after three days and nights there is
the first sign of the embryo inside the egg. The yolk forms
and rises to the sharp end of the egg from where the egg
hatches. The heart appears, like a speck of blood, in the
white of the egg. It beats and moves with life. The life-part
of the chick is the white of the egg, and it is nourished by the
navel string connected to the yolk.

About the twentieth day, if you open the egg and touch
the chick it moves inside and chirps and is already covered
with down feathers. After the twentieth day is past, the
chick begins to break the shell. Its head lies over its right leg
which it protects by covering it with its wing. The yolk
gets smaller and smaller until it is used up so that 10 days
after hatching, if you cut open the chick, a small part of the
yolk still remains inside the chick connected to its gut.

149

A catfish

A common ancestor?

Aristotle was also interested in fish. He remarked that some fish produce sounds by rubbing their gills and use this to communicate. He observed the shock in the sting of the torpedo fish, though he had no knowledge of electricity. Some of Aristotle's discriptions, however, were so far ahead of their time that he was laughed at by people who said he was inventing 'stories'. Here is one of them about the breeding habits of catfish.

The catfish lays its eggs in shallow water close to the roots of water plants or reeds. The sticky eggs cling to the reeds. When the female catfish lays her eggs, she goes away. The male remains and guards the eggs keeping away any other little fish who try to steal them. He does this for 40 or 50 days until the young catfish can look after themselves.

This unusual practice of the male catfish 'mothering' its young was disbelieved right up to 1856 when Louis Agassiz (a biologist) confirmed this. The fish is now named after Aristotle—*Parasiluris Aristotelis*.

Aristotle gave an interesting picture of the ape, comparing him to man.

The face of the ape resembles man in many ways; it has similar nostrils and ears and teeth like men, both front teeth and molars. It has eyelashes like men. Other animals have no under-eyelashes at all. The ape has arms like man, only covered with hair. His hands and fingers are like man. The ape's feet are very unusual. They are like hands and the toes are like fingers with middle one the longest. The under part of its foot is like a hand but very long and unusually hard at the back which resembles a heel.

150

When he studied man, Aristotle pointed out the relationship between his intelligence and his hand:

Many people believe that man is constructed faultily and inferior to other animals. He is barefooted, naked, and with no means of his own to defend himself. The other animals, however have only one method of defence, which they can never change. Man can defend himself in many ways, because his hand has many uses. It can be adapted for the use of a spear or sword or anything else. This comes about from its power of grasping and holding.

Aristotle's work in biology was so important that it influenced every person who studied biology after him. It is perhaps true to say that no major advance was made in the study of animals until Charles Darwin published his book about the subject of evolution. Even Darwin openly confessed how much he owed to Aristotle's research. The following letter to one of his friends shows this quite clearly:

February 22nd, 1882

My Dear Mr Ogle,

You must let me thank you for the pleasure which the introduction to the Aristotle book has given me. I have rarely read anything which has interested me more. . . . From the quotations which I had seen, I had a high notion of Aristotle's merits, but I had not the most remote notion what a wonderful man he was. Linnaeus and Cuvier (two biologists) have been my two gods . . . but they were mere schoolboys compared to old Aristotle. . . . I never realized, before reading the book, to what an enormous summation of labour we owe even our common knowledge. . . .

Yours very sincerely,
Charles Darwin

Botany (the study of plants)

The 'father' of botany was Theophrastus (372–288 BC), who was one of Aristotle's pupils. When Aristotle left Athens, he appointed Theophrastus as his successor in charge of the 'Lyceum' or university, which he had established. For thirty-five years Theophrastus continued the research which Aristotle had begun. He was interested in all kinds of subjects, but his particular interest lay in botany.

Fortunately for Theophrastus, the garden around the Lyceum contained a large number of different types of plants. Many of the plants had been sent back from the East by Alexander the Great when he was extending his empire. It was to

151

some extent a botanic garden and it was this which attracted him to study botany.

The Greeks before Theophrastus' time were interested in plants simply for food or medicine. Theophrastus was more interested in plants for their own sake. He wanted to find out the differences among plants, how they live, grow, and multiply, and what causes them to be there in the first place. He did all this in great detail.

> Since our knowledge is clearest when we are dealing with objects divided into classes, then we ought to divide everything into classes as much as possible.

Theophrastus was so fond of the garden of the Lyceum where he studied and its plants, that he requested to be buried there when he died:

> I hope that the person who lives there, will keep it and everything else in the same condition as before.

Things to do:

1 Who was the 'father' of biology?
2 Compare the expressions shown on the pictures of the ape with any of your own photographs.
3 Name the scientific fact discovered by Aristotle which was laughed at, but was later proved to be true.
4 What connection did Aristotle have with Charles Darwin?
5 Who was the 'father' of botany?
6 What relationship did he have with Aristotle?

Mathematics

What is mathematics? It is the science which deals with how numbers are related to each other and how different parts of space fit together. The great pioneer in discovering rules about these relationships was Pythagoras of Samos (566–497 BC).

His method was quite simple. He experimented with pebbles on the sand, trying to group them into different patterns such as squares, rectangles, and triangles. From this he was able to work out how many pebbles would fill a given pattern, and thereby the rules about the relationships of numbers.

Square numbers

Pythagoras experimented with the odd numbers, 1, 3, 5, 7, . . .

Starting with the number 1, he put round it the next odd number 3, in the shape of the letter L, to form a square pattern. He continued this process to form other squares:

Square Numbers
   1   4   9   16
The fourth square number (16) is made up of 4 rows each of 4 pebbles.

   ∴ The fourth square number is $4 \times 4 = 16$

   What is the fifth square number?

Rectangle numbers

Pythagoras used the same method with the even numbers, 2, 4, 6, 8, ... and this time he formed rectangles:

Rectangle Numbers
   2   6   12   20
The fourth rectangle number (20) is made up of 4 rows each of 5 pebbles.

   ∴ The fourth rectangle number is $4 \times 5 = 20$

   What is the fifth rectangle number?

Triangle numbers

Experimenting with the natural numbers 1, 2, 3, 4, ... Pythagoras discovered that by adding any number of them successively, they formed triangles:

Triangle Numbers
   1   3   6   10
The first four triangle numbers are 1, 3, 6, 10. What is the

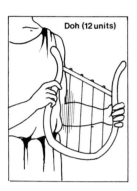

seventh triangle number? One way is to make the seventh triangle, then count all the pebbles in it. Pythagoras, however, discovered an easier way. He found out that the triangle number was simply half the rectangle number as shown below:

$$\text{The seventh rectangle number} = 7 \times 8 = 56$$

$$\therefore \text{The seventh triangle number} = \frac{7 \times 8}{2} = 28$$

Pythagoras soon became convinced after these discoveries that everything was made up of numbers. It was this which led him to discover mathematical proportion in music. He noticed that four strings of the lengths 12 : 9 : 8 : 6 produced the pleasant sounds—doh : me : soh : doh.

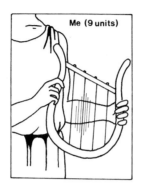

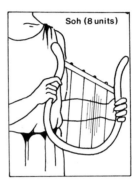

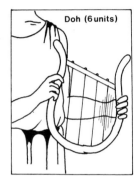

The four numbers are in geometric proportion:

$$\frac{12}{9} = \frac{8}{6}$$

The three numbers 12 : 8 : 6 are in what Pythagoras called 'harmonic' proportion:

> By whatever part of itself the first number is greater than the second, the second number is greater than the third by the same part of the third.

These are the notes which every pianist or guitarist plays to 'harmonize' with a singer or other instrument.

It was Pythagoras who found out rules of how patterns in space fit together, i.e. geometry. Working with right-angled triangles, he proved that the square on the side opposite the right-angle is equal to the sum of the squares on the other two sides.

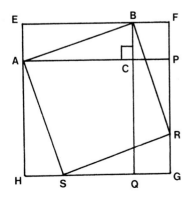

Given the figure left, Pythagoras proved that the square on AB = square on AC + square on CB. He considered the figure above from two different aspects:

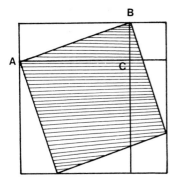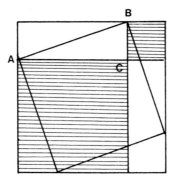

$AB^2 + 4$ triangles $= AC^2 + CB^2 + 2$ rectangles
but 4 triangles $= 2$ rectangles
$\therefore AB^2 = AC^2 + CB^2$

Pythagoras' method of experiment and observation profoundly influenced the minds of the Greek mathematicians who lived after him. It can be seen in the geometry books of Euclid of Alexandria (330–283 BC) which were studied in schools right through the Middle Ages to the present day. In the following illustration Euclid proves that the biggest angle in a triangle lies opposite the biggest side. This might seem obvious to us, but to the mathematician it first required proof.

'Let us suppose,' said Euclid, 'we have a triangle ABC with AC bigger than AB. Then we shall prove that angle ABC is bigger than angle ACB. Make AD equal to AB and join BD.

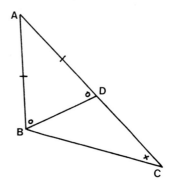

Proof: angle ADB = (because triangle ABD is an isosceles
        angle ABD   triangle)
        angle ADB is bigger than angle ACB (because angle
           ADB lies outside triangle BCD, and it
           has already been shown by a former
           proof that any angle lying outside a
           triangle is bigger than the interior
           opposite angle of that triangle).
      $\therefore$ angle ABD is bigger than angle ACB
      $\therefore$ angle ABC is bigger than angle ACB

so in every triangle, the bigger angle is opposite the bigger side. This is what we had to prove.'

Pythagoras' influence can also be seen in the work of Archimedes of Syracuse (287–212 BC). Archimedes was not only a great mathematician, but he was also an ingenious inventor. He invented the water-screw which, turning in a tightly fitted cylinder, could raise water from a river to irrigate the fields around. This led him to another invention—the bolt, which is a screw with a nut added to it. He worked out the rules about the lever. 'Give me a fulcrum', he said, 'and I will lift the earth.' Working with circles, he noticed that, if he measured the circumference of the circle, it was just slightly more than three times the size of the diameter. This relationship, which he described by the Greek letter π, he calculated to be $3\frac{1}{7}$ or 3·142 and is used in finding out the areas of circles. Perhaps his most famous discovery was in hydrostatics. Archimedes was taking a bath and when he raised his leg, he was surprised to notice that it was lighter than usual. From this he proceeded to prove, by experiments, that when a body is immersed in a liquid, its weight is lessened by the weight of the water displaced; when a body floats, its weight is equal to the weight of the liquid displaced.

His discovery was soon put to the test. The King of Syracuse suspected that his craftsmen had stolen some gold intended for his crown and had alloyed the remainder with silver to cover up the theft. Archimedes was asked to investigate.

Archimedes

After working out how much water a fixed amount of gold and silver would displace when immersed in the water, he is said to have exclaimed—'Eureka'—(I've got it) and the craftsmen were freed from their charge.

Archimedes was killed by a Roman solider during the siege of Syracuse while he was trying to solve some problem which he had set himself. His discoveries and inventions, however, continued to fire the minds of many others who came after him.

156

Things to do:

1 Copy into your jotters the first four patterns for the square, rectangle, and triangle numbers. Now make the patterns for the fifth and sixth square, rectangle and triangle numbers.

2 12 : 8 : 6 are 'harmonic' numbers.
Which notes do these lengths of string produce in a musical scale?

3 Draw and colour the two figures at the top of page 155 on a spare piece of paper. With a pair of scissors cut out the four uncoloured triangles in the figure on the left. Place them now over the two uncoloured rectangles on the figure on the right.

4 What relationship did Pythagoras discover about the sides in a right-angled triangle?

5 Make a list of some of the things discovered by Archimedes.

Philosophy

Who am I? Where did I come from? Where did the earth come from? Why am I on this earth? Where shall I go when I die? Why should I love my neighbour? Why should I not steal when I want to? What is a good person? Questions such as these have always puzzled mankind. The earliest people believed that the Gods made the earth and people on it; the Gods also decided what was good or bad and where you would go after you died. For a long time this is what men believed until some people among the Greeks began to challenge the power and authority of the Gods. They tried to find out if nature and life existed independently of the Gods. The important feature of their approach was the use of Reason as opposed to acceptance of blind superstition in finding answers to these important questions about ourselves.

Thales of Miletus watched the Nile building land on the Delta. From this he formed the conclusion that the basic element of matter was water. This is not surprising for from water we have the three states of matter, solid (ice), liquid (water) and gas (steam). Thales went on to suggest that since this was so, it was water that was responsible for the changes that occur around us and everything depends on and comes from water. This observation of Thales was the first great breakthrough. It was arrived at by the use of reason and it tried to show that what happens around us can be explained by natural causes and not by the will of some God as before.

This viewpoint of his, however, was soon taken up by others and modified.

Heraclitus declared that fire was the basic element because through its action all things changed.

Empelocles suggested that 'love' and 'strife' were the basic causes of all things since 'love' brought them together and 'strife' tore them apart.

Anaxagoras put forward the theory that it was rotating motion that was the cause of everything—a theory which recent astronomers have taken up.

Democritus of Abdera stated that everything was made up of exceedingly small indestructible particles—'atoms' which floated about in space until they joined together by some motion. This was basically an explanation of the 'Atomic Theory' which was brought back to life 100 years ago by Dalton when he reintroduced the idea of chemical balance and modern scientists agree that matter is made up of 'atoms'.

The observations of these thinkers very seriously challenged the old ideas about the Gods and their responsibility and power over everything. These men could give good scientific or natural causes for everything happening and changing, and if their theories might seem questionable, their approach based on sound reason was very difficult to ignore. Very soon other thinkers began to question the reasons why they should act in a certain way, why something should be good or bad, why they should do this and not that. They tried to look inside themselves and find answers to the questions—'Who am I? Why should I not steal when I want to? What makes a man good or bad?' In this type of enquiry the three great men tower above all others—Socrates, Plato and Aristotle.

Socrates was born in 469 BC. His father was a sculptor and his mother was a midwife. He applied himself to having no needs and in order to be freer lived on little, walked barefooted summer and winter, wearing only a shabby coat; the anger of the people had no more effect upon him than heat or cold on his body.

He concerned himself mainly with the thoughts and behaviour of himself and his fellow humans. The purpose of his life was to convert others to virtue and truth by asking questions and attempting to find answers.

The following is an extract of a conversation Socrates had with his friend Euthyphro where he tries to find out why we should say that it is right to do something:

SOCRATES: By Zeus, Euthyphro, do you really think that you are so sure about what makes a thing sacred? Tell me then what makes a thing right and sacred and what makes a thing wicked and not sacred!

EUTHYPHRO: Well, I have been saying just now that what I am doing at this moment is right namely taking a person to court who does wrong whether it be your father or mother or anyone else, and not to do this is wicked.

SOCRATES: What you are saying is partly right and partly not. What I have just asked you I shall try to say more clearly. When I asked you, my good friend, you did not explain to me quite clearly enough what makes a thing right. You simply told me that what you are now doing happens to be right, that is accusing your father of murder.

EUTHYPHRO: Yes, Socrates, what you say is the truth.

SOCRATES: Perhaps. Now then do you say that many other things are right?

EUTHYPHRO: Yes, that is so.

SOCRATES: But do you not see that this is not the question I asked you 'will you—explain to me one or two of the many things that are right?' The actual question I asked was this—'if a thing is right, what makes it right? or if a thing is sacred, what makes it sacred?' For it is one single thing that makes what is right to be right and to be completely opposite to what is wicked and the same is the case for what is sacred and what is not sacred.

Do you not agree that this is so?

EUTHYPHRO: Yes, that is quite true.

Plato, *Euthyphro* 5–7

Plato

Naturally many of his questions began to disturb people who thought that he was being too critical of their religion. The result was that he was accused of corrupting people and was forced to kill himself by drinking hemlock, a poisonous drug.

Plato, who was the pupil of Socrates, recorded much of what Socrates said and discovered. He was inspired by his master's genius and continued the good work. He was physically strong, wrestled, wrote poems, had a vast library, studied all the known sciences, with an absorbing desire for truth.

Ten years after Socrates died he travelled through Egypt and Libya and visited Italy but soon returned to Athens where he set up a school which became famous and attracted young men from all over the Greek world. As a brilliant mathematician and scientist he was able to apply his great mind to these eternal questions about man's attitudes, what makes him do this or that, how people should govern, what the laws should con-

Aristotle

sists of. His books *The Republic* and *The Laws* are still studied today.

Aristotle (the pupil of Plato) 384–322 BC wrote 'all men possess by nature the desire to know' and this sums up his whole attitude to life—to know, to learn.

He too, like Plato, formed a school in Athens called the Lyceum where he taught for twelve years. At the age of 62 he died with a stomach complaint brought on by overwork. He wrote over 200 books on all types of subjects. He tried to explain what was happening all around him by the use of reason rather than by blind superstition as before. He was outstanding in his work on Logic or correct reasoning and by setting forth the steps to be used in doing so.

Like Plato he shared the great idea of Socrates that 'unexamined life is not the life for a man. It must continually be inspected and re-inspected.'

Things to do:

1 Write a paragraph about each of the following: Socrates; Plato; Aristotle.
2 Find out about some of the great 'Thinkers' of today.

12 Alexander the Great

Statue of Alexander

Alexander the Great

One of the greatest soldiers of all time was Alexander the Great. When he died at the age of thirty-three he had conquered most of the world known to his contemporaries. It was due to his conquests that Greek culture and Greek learning spread far beyond the bounds of Greece.

Macedonia

Alexander was king of Macedonia in northern Greece. The Macedonians looked upon themselves as Greeks and spoke Greek, but the Greeks of the south called them barbarians and declared that they could not understand what they said. King Philip, Alexander's father, was a great admirer of Greek civilization and culture. He studied Greek literature and Greek art. It was his ambition to lead a united army of Greeks against the Persians and so keep Greece free for ever. But to do this he had first to build up an army strong enough to control all Greece. This army was to become one of the most feared military forces in the Ancient World.

The main body of infantry formed what is called a Phalanx. This was a solid body of between eight and nine thousand men. Each soldier was armed with a spear measuring thirteen to twenty-four feet in length, so that a solid wall of steel faced the enemy. This solid body of men would keep the front of the enemy engaged while Philip's cavalry attacked the enemy flanks. His cavalry included a band of noble Macedonians known as his 'Companions', who later under Alexander, numbered two thousand, and with him attacked the enemy in battle. With this army Philip set out to gain control of Greece. He faced considerable opposition from cities such as Thebes and Athens. We can still read the speeches which the great orator Demosthenes made, calling upon the citizens of Athens to go out and resist Philip before it was too late.

Demosthenes

Philip cannot rest content with what he has conquered, he is always taking in more, everywhere casting his net round us, while we sit idle and do nothing. When, Athenians, will you take the necessary action? What are you waiting for? Tell me, are you content to run round and ask each other 'Is there any news today?'? Could there be any news more startling than that a Macedonian is triumphing over Athenians and settling the destiny of Greece?

But all opposition was crushed at the battle of Chaeronea where Philip was victorious over the Athenians and Thebans, thanks partly to the courage of Alexander and his 'Companions'.

Philip now prepared to lead the Greeks against the Persian Empire but before his plans could be carried out he was murdered and his son Alexander, a youth of twenty, succeeded him.

Alexander's boyhood

Alexander's mother believed that she was descended from Achilles, and she encouraged her son to try to do even greater deeds than his famous ancestor. When Alexander was thirteen years old, his father Philip had invited the famous teacher Aristotle to educate him. Alexander became greatly interested in science, especially in medicine and nature study and in Greek literature and Greek ways. He is said to have known the Iliad by heart and to have slept with a copy of this poem (and a dagger) under his pillow.

Alexander and his tutor Aristotle
(from the film *Alexander the Great*)

162

One day, when Alexander was still a boy, a horse dealer brought to the court of Macedon a magnificent horse named Bucephalus, which he offered to sell for a vast sum of money. When the king's horsemen tried to mount Bucephalus, the horse kicked and bucked so much that the king ordered the dealer to take it away. Alexander asked permission to try to ride the horse; when it was granted he turned Bucephalus to face the sun before leaping up on its back and riding him away. He had noticed that Bucephalus was afraid of his own shadow. In this way he gained the horse on which he led the Greeks against the Persian Empire.

| | Macedonia when Philip became King |
| | Macedonia when Philip Died |

Alexander rides Bucephalus into battle *(left)*

Even as a young lad Alexander was eager for glory, and when he heard of a great victory gained by his father, or of a town that had been subdued by him, he was more sorry than glad, and said to his companions, 'My father will make so many conquests that there will be nothing left for me to win.'

The invasion of Persia

When Alexander became king, he decided to continue his

163

Greek fighting Persian

father's plan of attacking Persia. He wished to do this because Persia was still a threat to Greece's freedom. Alexander's first act after crossing the Hellespont was to go to Troy and there to lay a garland on the tomb of Achilles. He than marched to the River Granicus where Darius, king of the Persians, was waiting with a force stronger than Alexander's. Alexander charged across the river on his horse at the head of his 'Companions'. He could be distinguished by a large plume of white feathers on his helmet. The Persians made for him and one of them almost killed him with his scimitar, but his friend Cleitus struck it aside and saved his life. Then with the help of the phalanx the Persians were overcome.

After capturing Sardis he marched southwards along the coast so as to deprive the Persian fleet of its bases and to leave Greece safe from invasion. Then marching inland, he came to the town of Gordium in Asia Minor where there was a chariot which had belonged to Gordius an early king of that town. The yoke of this chariot was tied with a knot which nobody had been able to untie. An oracle had declared that whoever untied this knot would reign over all Asia. When Alexander was told this he said, 'Thus I will perform the task', and with one stroke of his sword he cut the knot. The phrase 'to cut the Gordian knot' is still used for solving a complicated difficulty in a direct and simple way.

Success after success followed. Darius was defeated at Issus and though he escaped himself, his wife and his mother fell into Alexander's hands.

Alexander conquered Tyre and marched into Egypt where he was welcomed by the Egyptians who chose him as their king and believed he was the son of their great god Amun. On some of his coins Alexander is shown with ram's horns, the sign of Amun, in his hair. In Egypt he founded the famous city of Alexandria which still bears his name.

In the last battle against Alexander at Gaugamela the Persian king thought that he had found the answer to the superiority of the Macedonian phalanx. He had sharp scythes fitted to the wheels of his chariots to cut down the Greeks. But Alexander's archers and javelin throwers succeeded in killing many charioteers. Then the soldiers of the phalanx quickly opened their ranks and let the chariots pass harmlessly through them. Then when a gap appeared in the Persian line Alexander and his 'Companions' charged. They made straight for Darius. The Persian king turned and fled.

As Alexander marched on Babylon the people, led by their priests, came to welcome him as king. Susa, the second big city, also surrendered and gave up its treasures. But the city

Coin showing the head of Alexander wearing the horns of Amun

Alexander's route through Asia Minor and Egypt

called 'the richest of all the cities under the sun' was Persepolis in the highlands of Persia. Alexander entered this city after a battle and found so much treasure that twenty thousand mules and five thousand camels were required to carry it away. When he had looted Persepolis, Alexander burned the city. Alexander now set off in pursuit of Darius. But by the time he caught up with him, the Persian king was dead, murdered by one of his own generals.

Discontent among the soldiers

So far Alexander's soldiers had followed him willingly. He shared their dangers and toils, and they all had a share in the treasures which were captured. But now a great scheme was forming in his mind, which they could not understand. He wanted to join the Persians and Greeks together in one Empire

165

The battle of Guagamela; the Greeks open ranks, allowing the Persian chariots to pass harmlessly through

The Khyber pass, near Peshawar

with himself as king. The Persians had always treated their king as a god, and they fell down on their faces before Alexander. To please them he sometimes appeared in Persian dress. He married Darius' daughter and at the same ceremony eighty of his officers married eighty noble Persian girls. His soldiers grumbled that Alexander was beginning to turn into a Persian. Alexander himself began to suspect some of his best friends of rebellion and had them put to death. One night at a banquet, in a drunken rage, he killed his friend Cleitus who had once saved his life in battle and he never afterwards forgave himself.

The Macedonians had for some time been wanting to march homeward rather than into new unknown lands. But Alexander marched on towards India. Wherever he went he founded new towns and named them after himself. In each town he left some soldiers who had to settle there and hold the place. He eventually reached the river Indus by way of Afghanistan and the Khyber Pass. Even the Indian king Porus, who was said to be seven feet tall and whose army included elephants, could not stop Alexander. In the battle against Porus, Alexander's horse Bucephalus was killed. Alexander later built a city on the battlefield and called it Bucephalon.

Now Alexander intended to march through northern India to the river Ganges which he believed to be the edge of the world. But his army refused to go any further. Ever since they had crossed the Indus rain had fallen incessantly. They were tired, many were wounded and they had not seen their homes for eight long years.

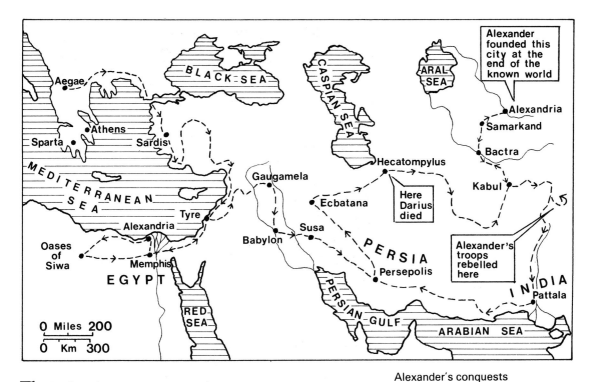

Alexander founded this city at the end of the known world

Here Darius died

Alexander's troops rebelled here

Alexander's conquests

The return

Alexander had to promise to take them back to Persia. However, he would not return by the way he had already travelled. So he marched back through new country, which turned out to be mostly desert, where many of his men died of thirst and

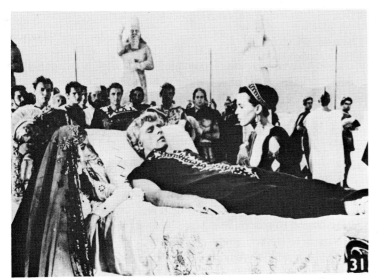

The death of Alexander (from the film *Alexander the Great*)

hunger and weariness. Some of the army he had sent back by sea, in ships they had built in India. When they had returned to Babylon, Alexander was struck down with fever and died at the age of thirty-three.

What Alexander achieved

Alexander had won all his battles, founded a great many new towns and made himself ruler of a vast empire. As soon as he died his empire was divided among the most powerful of his generals, and they quarrelled and fought over their possessions until another great power appeared which conquered Greece and took over the lands which Alexander had ruled. This new power was Rome. What had Alexander achieved? He had opened up a new world, just as Columbus did many hundreds of years later. He revealed to the Greeks a great wide world beyond their own small inward looking city states and to the inhabitants of this new world he gave the ideas and the culture of the Greeks. It was the dawn of the Hellenistic Age when Greek knowledge spread throughout the East because of the new cities Alexander had built wherever he had conquered.

The legend of Alexander has been handed down to posterity in many different countries. Stories about him have been found in twenty-four different languages. Tribes on the slopes of the Hindu Kush claim descent from him. His story still grips the imagination of men.

Things to do:

Write down the heading *Alexander the Great*. Underline it.

Section A

1 Copy down the following paragraph completing the sentences.

Alexander the Great was king of .... He led his army against the Persian Empire because .... He defeated King .... in several battles, the final one being fought at .... After completing the conquest of the Persian Empire, Alexander turned south and headed into .... He hoped to reach the river .... His soldiers, however refused to go any further because .... Alexander had to return to Babylon and there he died of .... at the age of ....

2 Explain what is meant by:
  (a) Phalanx; (b) Alexander's 'Companions'.

Section B
1 Do you think that Alexander the Great lived a worthwhile life? Write a paragraph to justify your answer.
2 Write a letter from one of Alexander's soldiers home to his wife telling her about the army's adventures.
3 Find out from a reference book about:
  (a) The Pharos of Alexandria; (b) Achilles.
4 Consult an atlas and list the modern names of the countries which came under Alexander's control.
5 Draw a picture of:
  (a) a battle scene between Greeks and Persians; *or*
  (b) Alexander taming Bucephalus; *or*
  (c) Alexander on his death bed.

Acknowledgments

The Publisher's thanks are due to the following for permission to reproduce copyright material:
Banta for the illustration Chick Embryo from Set 17, Bioviewers and Biosets; Hodder & Stoughton Ltd for an extract from A. R. Burn's *History of Greece*; Penguin Books Ltd for extracts from Thucydides: *The History of the Peloponnesian War*, tr. Rex Warner, Herodotus: *The Histories*, tr. Aubrey de Selincourt, © The Estate of Aubrey de Selincourt (1954), Aeschylus: *The Persians* from *Prometheus Bound and Other Plays*, tr. Philip Vellacott, © Philip Vellacott (1961) and Aristophanes: *The Poet and the Women* from *The Frogs and Other Plays*, tr. David Barrett, © David Barrett (1964); Oxford University Press for extracts from Plato's *Portrait of Socrates*, tr. Sir Richard Livingstone (1938); The Loeb Classical Library (Harvard University Press: William Heinmann) for extracts from Xenophon's *Oeconomicus* and Demosthenes (*page 162*) and Centaur Books Ltd for diagrams from Wilkie's *Ancient Models*.

The Publisher's thanks are also due to the following for permission to reproduce copyright photographs:
National Tourist Office of Greece: pp. 1, 13, 22, 29. *Camera Press*: pp. 5 (top, Jon Blau, bottom, Bernard G. Silberstein), 6 (Geraldine Kenway), 56 (Len Sirman), 160 (Len Sirman), 161 (Turgat Mantar). *Mansell Collection*: pp. 11, 14, 17 (top), 20, 26 (right), 49, 116 (bottom left), 128, 129, 134, 136, 159, 162 (left), 163, 164 (bottom). *Documentation Photographique de la Réunion des Musées Nationaux/Louvre*: p. 15 (top), *British Library*: p. 15 (bottom). *British Museum*: pp. 16 (top), 42, 73 (top right), 80, 81 (top), 82 (left), 92 (top right), 116 (right), 125. *Metropolitan Museum of Art, New York*: pp. 17 (bottom), 18 (bottom), 79, 86, 92 (bottom left and right), 93 (top right) 96, 116 (top left). *Fitzwilliam Museum, Cambridge*: p. 18 (top left). *National Archaeological Museum, Athens*: pp. 18 (top right), 32, 51 (bottom). *Staatliche Museen zu Berlin*: pp. 19, 26 (bottom left). *Glyptothek, Munich*: p. 23 (top). *Janet March-Penny*: pp. 23 (bottom), 110, 111 (bottom right). *Museum of Fine Arts, Boston*: pp. 24, 26 (top left), 93 (left), 97, 103 (bottom left), 124 (top), 126 (bottom). *Visual Publications*: p. 38. *American School of Classical Studies, Athens*: pp. 44, 88, 130 (right and left), 131. *Bildarchiv Preussischer Kulturbesitz*: pp. 50, 103 (right), 105 (top and bottom), 115. *Popperfoto*: pp. 51 (top), 111 (bottom left). *Iran Bastan Museum/Iranian Centre for Archaeological Research*: p. 53. *Alinari*: p. 55. *U.S. Department of the Interior, National Parks Service*: p. 74 (right). *Glasgow Herald/Evening Times*: pp. 60 (bottom), 74 (top left). *BBC*: p. 61. *Smith*: p. 68. *P. Gallias*: pp. 72, 73 (top left), 73 (bottom). *Irish Tourist Board*: p. 74 (bottom left). *Ministry of Culture and Science, Athens*: p. 81 (bottom). *Soprintendenza alle Antichita, Calabria, Italy*: p. 82 (right). *E. W. Tattersall*: p. 84 (left and right). *Michael Holford*: pp. 100, 117 (top and bottom). *Musée du Louvre et M. Chuzeville*: pp. 111 (top left), 124 (bottom). *Robert Harding & Associates*: p. 111 (top right). *Ashmolean Museum, Oxford*: p. 126 (top). *Controller of Her Majesty's Stationery Office, Crown copyright*: p. 133. *Spectrum*: p. 135. *John R. Freeman & Co.*: p. 147. *Courtesy Educational Productions, Ltd.*: pp. 162 (right), 166 (top), 167. *Oxford University Press*: p. 164 (top). *High Commissioner for Pakistan*: p. 166 (bottom); *D. A. Harissidis*: pp. 28, 98; *Forth Studios, Edinburgh*: p. 60 (top).